# American
# Headway

**WORKBOOK 4**

## THE WORLD'S MOST TRUSTED ENGLISH COURSE

**SECOND EDITION**

**John and Liz Soars**
**Sylvia Wheeldon**

Spotlight on Testing lessons
by Lawrence J. Zwier

## OXFORD
UNIVERSITY PRESS

# Contents

You will need to listen to the Student Workbook CD for some exercises. If you do not have the Student Workbook CD, you can access the audio files on the *American Headway* Student Audio Download Center or read the Audio Scripts on pp. 81–85.

# 1 No place like home

**Grammar:** The tense system
**Vocabulary:** Compound nouns • *house* and *home* idioms
**Pronunciation:** Vowel sounds

## The tense system

▶▶ **Grammar Reference 1.2 Student Book pp. 136–137**

### 1 Identifying tenses

**1** Complete the sentences with the correct active or passive form of the verbs in the boxes.

| walk |

1. **A** How did you get here?
   **B** We __walked_____. It didn't take long.

2. Our baby Jack _____ now. He's just a year old.

3. I need to rest. We _____ nonstop for four hours.

| take |

4. It was a hard game. At halftime, one of the players _____ to the hospital.

5. I'm exhausted. I think I _____ a break.

6. My dog looked guilty. He _____ some food from the kitchen table.

| have |

7. We need a new car. We _____ this one for years.

8. We _____ a perfect picnic until my wife was stung by a bee.

9. Don't call at 8:00 tomorrow. We _____ breakfast then.

| make |

10. Our sandwiches _____ fresh every day.

11. Have you heard about Lenny? He _____ CEO of the company.

12. By the time I'm 40, I _____ enough money to retire.

| wash |

13. **A** Where are my jeans?
    **B** They _____ right now.

14. My favorite white T-shirt turned pink. It _____ with my daughter's red sweater.

15. His shirt was all wet because he _____ the car.

| sell |

16. She likes her job. She _____ cars.

17. If no one offers to buy the house, it _____ at auction next month.

18. I wish I'd bought that antique chair I saw in the store window. I'm sure it _____ by now.

| teach |

19. At the end of the semester I _____ for six years.

20. The children _____ how to make cookies when a boy dropped his bowl on the teacher's foot.

**2** Complete the tense chart with the verb forms from Exercise 1.

| Active | Simple | Continuous |
|---|---|---|
| Present | | |
| Past | walked | |
| Future | | |
| Present Perfect | | |
| Past Perfect | | |
| Future Perfect | | |
| **Passive** | **Simple** | **Continuous** |
| Present | | |
| Past | | |
| Future | | |
| Present Perfect | | |
| Past Perfect | | |
| Future Perfect | will have been sold | |

## 2 Correcting mistakes

Correct the sentences.

*'m working*

1. I ~~work~~ hard these days because I have exams next week.

2. It's really cold lately, so I've bought a new winter coat.

3. The Yankees play really well this season. Their new player has real talent.

4. I've heard you'll have a baby! Congratulations.

5. I was doing my homework when my friend was calling.

6. When I was a little girl, I've always spent my allowance on candy.

7. I went out with Paulo for two years now, and we're still crazy about each other.

8. I can't decide what to buy my brother for his birthday. Maybe I'm going to get him a new shirt.

9. A one-day strike has called by the union for Friday this week.

10. The teacher said that Megan had been working hard and was deserved to pass all her tests.

## 3 Choosing the right tense

**CD 2** Read the telephone conversation between Teresa in Tanzania and her mother in the United States. Put the verbs in parentheses in the correct tense.

# Calling home

**M** Hello?

**T** Mom! It's me! How (1) __are__ you __doing__ (do)?

**M** Teresa! What a nice surprise! How is school?

**T** Actually, I (2) _____ (not teach) now. The school year (3) _____ (be) over, finally! Some friends and I (4) _____ (visit) Zanzibar Island. We (5) _____ (arrive) here by boat last night, and I just (6) _____ (find) this public phone, and I (7) _____ (want) to call you for a while, so …

**M** Well, it (8) _____ (be) great to hear your voice. Your father and I (9) _____ (miss) you so much. I'm glad you (10) _____ (come) home in a few weeks.

**T** Yeah, me too. But I (11) _____ (send) you lots of e-mails and letters, haven't I? I (12) _____ (write) you guys another long letter today, but it isn't finished yet. And I (13) _____ (buy) you some cool presents!

**M** Oh, that's wonderful. And I hope your dad and I (14) _____ (be able to) visit you the next time you go abroad.

**T** Yes, definitely. But, Mom, let me tell you about Zanzibar. I (15) _____ never _____ (see) such a beautiful place in all my life. This morning, we (16) _____ (go) to the most gorgeous white-sand beach. The water (17) _____ (feel) so warm, and there (18) _____ (not be) any other tourists around. Tomorrow, we (19) _____ (visit) the old markets in Zanzibar Town.

**M** Sounds amazing! Lucky you!

**T** Yes, but I (20) _____ really _____ (look forward) to coming home again and seeing you and Dad!

**M** Me too. We (21) _____ (wait) for you at the airport!

## Passives

▶▶ **Grammar Reference 1.2 Student Book p. 137**

### 4 Active or passive?

**1** These sentences sound unnatural in the active. Rewrite them using the passive.

1. They built our house in the 18th century.
   **Our house was built in the 18th century.**

2. Someone's decorating my apartment this month.
   _____

3. Has someone fixed the coffee maker yet?
   _____

4. While they were building the new kitchen, we ate in restaurants.
   While the new kitchen _____
   _____

5. On Monday morning they found out that someone had robbed the bank.
   _____

6. They won't recognize her in those dark glasses.
   She _____

**2** Put the verbs in parentheses into the correct tense, active or passive.

1. The thieves **were caught** (catch) as they **were leaving** (leave) the office.

2. The mail _____ (pick up) at 12:00 every day.

3. Aunt Mary is terribly upset. Her cat _____ (miss) for three days now.

4. We _____ (drive) down a quiet country road when suddenly we _____ (overtake) by a police car.

5. When I woke up this morning, the world looked magical. It _____ (snow) all night.

6. When you _____ (arrive) in New York tomorrow, you _____ (pick up) by one of our drivers and taken to the conference center.

# Living it up!

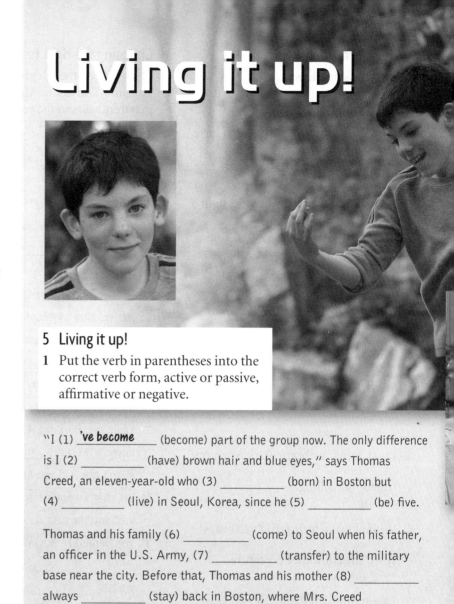

### 5 Living it up!

**1** Put the verb in parentheses into the correct verb form, active or passive, affirmative or negative.

"I (1) **'ve become** (become) part of the group now. The only difference is I (2) _____ (have) brown hair and blue eyes," says Thomas Creed, an eleven-year-old who (3) _____ (born) in Boston but (4) _____ (live) in Seoul, Korea, since he (5) _____ (be) five.

Thomas and his family (6) _____ (come) to Seoul when his father, an officer in the U.S. Army, (7) _____ (transfer) to the military base near the city. Before that, Thomas and his mother (8) _____ always _____ (stay) back in Boston, where Mrs. Creed (9) _____ (employed) in a university science lab.

Unlike other U.S. military children, Thomas (10) _____ (attend) a local Korean elementary school. He (11) _____ (enroll) here for six years. At first he (12) _____ (struggle) to learn Korean, but he (13) _____ (speak) it fluently now. "People (14) _____ (blow away) when they hear me speak because I'm obviously not Korean," he says. He (15) _____ even _____ (interview) in a local newspaper.

Thomas still (16) _____ (miss) some things from home, like American comic books. "You can get them here," he says, "but they (17) _____ all _____ (translate) into Korean. It's not the same."

Thomas (18) _____ (have) a lot of fun with his friends in Korea, but his parents (19) _____ (want) him to go to high school in the U.S. so he can (20) _____ (accept) by a good American college. "Who knows?" he says. "Maybe I (21) _____ (be) a translator one day!"

# Auxiliary verbs

▶▶ **Grammar Reference 1.1 Student Book p. 136**

## 6 *have, be,* or *do*?

Complete the sentences with the correct form of *have, be,* or *do*. Write **A** for an auxiliary verb and **F** for a full verb. Sometimes the auxiliary is negative.

1. [A] They **had** finished dinner when we arrived.
2. [F] We **had** pizza last night.
3. ☐ It _____ been a wonderful day. Thank you.
4. ☐ I _____ my homework very quickly yesterday.
5. ☐ I _____ so tired.
6. ☐ I _____ always had a passion for Indian food.
7. ☐ Jane _____ not at work today.
8. ☐ Tanya overslept, so she _____ catch her train.
9. ☐ What have you _____ to your hair? You look awful!
10. ☐ What _____ your new boyfriend look like?
11. ☐ This self-portrait _____ painted by Van Gogh.
12. ☐ My car is _____ repaired today.
13. ☐ I hate _____ the dishes. I'd like a dishwasher.
14. ☐ I've _____ doing this exercise for hours.

## 7 Missing auxiliaries in spoken English

Rewrite the underlined sentences with the missing words.

1. <u>Seen John?</u> I need to talk to him.

   **Have you seen John?** _____

2. <u>Staying late?</u> I have had enough. I'm going home.

   _____

3. <u>Talk to you later!</u>

   _____

4. <u>Going home?</u> Have a nice weekend.

   _____

5. <u>Heard the news?</u> Your candidate is the new president.

   _____

6. <u>Got a minute?</u> I need some help with my computer.

   _____

7. <u>Finished already?</u> That was quick.

   _____

8. <u>Want some help?</u> I don't have anything to do.

   _____

## 2 Here are the answers to some questions about Thomas Creed. Write the questions.

1. **Where was Thomas born** ?
   In Boston.

2. _____ ?
   To a military base near Seoul.

3. _____ ?
   In a university science lab.

4. What kind of _____ ?
   A local Korean elementary school.

5. _____ fluently now?
   Yes, he does.

6. _____ ?
   Because he's obviously not Korean.

7. Where _____ ?
   In a local newspaper.

8. _____ ?
   So he can be accepted by a good American college.

# Vocabulary

## 8 Compound nouns

The same word completes the three compound nouns in each box. Fill in the blanks with the letters of the words

1.
| b l o o d test |
| b l o o d pressure |
| b l o o d donor |

2.
| _ _ _ _ cover |
| _ _ _ _ mark |
| _ _ _ _ shelf |

3.
| _ _ _ _ _ fall |
| _ _ _ _ _ melon |
| _ _ _ _ _ skiing |

4.
| _ _ _ _ _ club |
| _ _ _ _ _ mare |
| _ _ _ _ _ time |

5.
| brief _ _ _ _ |
| suit _ _ _ _ |
| book _ _ _ _ |

6.
| tea _ _ _ |
| plastic _ _ _ |
| sleeping _ _ _ |

7.
| _ _ _ bow |
| _ _ _ _ coat |
| _ _ _ _ drop |

8.
| _ _ shine |
| _ _ rise |
| _ _ set |

9.
| _ _ _ _ side |
| _ _ _ _ sign |
| _ _ _ _ map |

10.
| _ _ light |
| _ _ break |
| _ _ dream |

11.
| _ _ _ _ shake |
| _ _ _ _ writing |
| _ _ _ _ bag |

12.
| _ _ _ cube |
| _ _ berg |
| _ _ _ rink |

13.
| birthday _ _ _ _ |
| credit _ _ _ _ |
| business _ _ _ _ |

14.
| _ _ _ _ scape |
| _ _ _ lady |
| _ _ _ slide |

*"Amazing! But when we go on vacation one suitcase is too heavy for you."*

## 9 *house* and *home* idioms

**1** Put a check (✔) next to the correct definition for each <u>underlined</u> sentence. Use a dictionary if necessary.

1. Help yourself to tea or coffee. <u>Make yourself at home.</u>
   a. ☐ Make your own drinks.
   b. ☐ Please behave in my house as if it were yours.

2. <u>The new Broadway musical brought the house down.</u> The producers are very happy.
   a. ☐ The musical was a success.
   b. ☐ The musical wasn't a success.

3. <u>The news report really brought home to me the horrors of the famine.</u>
   a. ☐ The report made me realize fully the horrors of the famine.
   b. ☐ The report clearly showed the horrors of famine.

4. <u>His sarcastic comments really hit home.</u> He shouldn't have said that.
   a. ☐ He was sarcastic about my house.
   b. ☐ His comments really hurt my feelings.

**2** Complete the conversations with the idioms from Exercise 1 in the correct form.

1. **A** I was so sorry to hear that your cat died.
   **B** Thank you. When I saw her empty bowl, it really _____ that I'd never see her again.

2. **A** Hello! Sorry we're so late. Our plane was delayed.
   **B** Don't worry. Just sit down and relax, and _____! I'll make some coffee.

3. **A** Did you read those excellent reviews in the local paper about the school play?
   **B** Yes, I did. Apparently, it _____!

4. **A** Why is Terence always so horrible to poor Janine?
   **B** I don't know, but I could see in her face that his criticisms really _____ this time. Maybe she'll finally leave him.

# Phrasal verbs

## 10 Literal and idiomatic meanings

 Phrasal verbs sometimes have a literal meaning, and sometimes an idiomatic meaning:

*I **looked up** the tree, but I couldn't see my cat.* (literal)

*I **looked up** the spelling in my dictionary.* (idiomatic)

**1** In this exercise the phrasal verbs are all used literally. Complete the sentences with the particles from the box. Some are used more than once.

> away   on   off   back   out   down   in

1. The dentist said my tooth was bad. He had to pull it **out**_____.

2. Don't run _____! Come here! I want to talk to you.

3. My aunt fell _____ the stairs and broke her leg.

4. And I fell _____ my horse!

5. When the sun went _____ it was really cold.

6. A button has come _____ my shirt. Could you sew it back _____ for me?

7. I don't feel like cooking tonight. What about eating _____?

8. I'm going to the library to take _____ the books I've finished.

9. I've just hung the laundry out, and it's starting to rain. Can you help me to bring it _____?

10. Don't throw that empty box _____. I'm sure I can use it for something.

**2** Complete the pairs of sentences with the same phrasal verb from the box in the correct form. Write *L* for a literal meaning and *I* for an idiomatic one.

> take off    come up    pick up
> put up     put down    hold on

1. ☑L The sun was **coming up**_____ when we woke up.

   ☑I They will let me know if any issues **come up**_____.

2. ☐ Could you _____ me _____ tonight? I don't have any other place to sleep.

   ☐ It's October 30 already. We have to _____ the Halloween decorations.

3. ☐ Please _____ the box _____ on the floor.

   ☐ She _____ him _____ with her remarks. He had never been so humiliated in his life.

4. ☐ **A** Can I speak to Kate, please?

   **B** _____. I'll get her.

   ☐ When you're riding on the back of a motorcycle, you have to _____ tight.

5. ☐ It's too warm to be wearing a sweater. Why don't you _____ it _____?

   ☐ After a slow start, my business finally started to _____.

6. ☐ I was never taught how to cook. I just _____ it _____ from my mother.

   ☐ The baby's crying. Can you _____ him _____?

# Pronunciation

## 11 Vowel sounds

**CD 3** Write the words from the box in the correct place in the chart.

| | | |
|---|---|---|
| letter | busy | tree |
| suit | good | fun |
| sock | camp | early |
| floor | father | weather |
| woman | more | father |
| work | women | shoe |
| heat | mother | score |
| cool | machine | building |
| odd | breakfast | family |
| could | accent | thumb |

| / u / | / ʊ / |
|---|---|
| suit | good |

| / ʌ / | / ər / |
|---|---|
| fun | early |

| / ɔr / | / ɑ / |
|---|---|
| floor | sock |

| / æ / | / ɛ / |
|---|---|
| camp | letter |

| / ɪ / | / i / |
|---|---|
| busy | tree |

# Listening

## 12 A good friend

1  **CD 4** Listen to the conversation. Mark the sentences true (✔) or false (✗).

1. ☒ Maggie and Jenny arranged to meet.
2. ☐ Maggie has been away.
3. ☐ Jenny's enjoying work these days.
4. ☐ Jenny likes her new boss.
5. ☐ Jenny doesn't want to apply for another job.
6. ☐ Jenny and Sam have enough money for a new car.
7. ☐ Jenny is going to convince Sam that Maggie needs a vacation.
8. ☐ Jenny is grateful to Maggie.

2  **CD 4** Listen again. Find the informal expressions that match these definitions.

1. visit someone unexpectedly _____
2. Tell me what you have been doing. _____
3. all day, every day _____
4. not be in the mood for something _____
5. isn't enjoyable or good _____
6. unable to tolerate _____

3  Look at the audio script on page 81. Find examples of where words are missing in informal conversation.

# 2 Been there, done that!

**Grammar:** Present Perfect—Simple or Continuous?
**Vocabulary:** *make* or *do*? • Travel and transportation
**Pronunciation:** Word stress

## Present Perfect

▶▶ **Grammar Reference 2.1 Student Book pp. 137–138**

### 1 Present Perfect Simple or Continuous?

**1** Match a line in **A** with a line in **B** to make sentences.

| A | B |
|---|---|
| 1. [a] I've written<br>2. ☐ I've been writing | a. to Fay to wish her happy birthday.<br>b. my essay all morning. |
| 3. ☐ I've lost<br>4. ☐ I've been losing | c. weight recently.<br>d. my car keys. |
| 5. ☐ They've missed<br>6. ☐ They've been missing | e. you lots, so come home soon.<br>f. the train. |
| 7. ☐ She's been talking<br>8. ☐ She's talked | g. on the phone for hours.<br>h. about this subject before. |
| 9. ☐ Paula's been leaving<br>10. ☐ Paula's left | i. her company.<br>j. work late everyday this week. |
| 11. ☐ The cat's been going<br>12. ☐ The cat's gone | k. to our neighbor's to have his dinner lately.<br>l. upstairs. Please bring him back. |
| 13. ☐ He's had<br>14. ☐ He's been having | m. a heart attack.<br>n. second thoughts about accepting the job. |
| 15. ☐ I've been saving up<br>16. ☐ I've saved up | o. to buy a new television.<br>p. about $200. |
| 17. ☐ I've been swimming<br>18. ☐ I've swum | q. 20 lengths today.<br>r. , which is why my hair is wet. |
| 19. ☐ I've been finding<br>20. ☐ I've found | s. my checkbook at last.<br>t. it difficult to concentrate recently. |

**2** Put the verbs in parentheses into the Present Perfect Simple or Continuous.

1. I **'ve been playing** (play) tennis all morning, and I'm really tired.

2. Please drive carefully to work. It _____, (snow) and the roads are very dangerous.

3. How far _____ you _____ (travel) this morning?

4. Kay and Bruno _____ (live) in Boston for the past five years. Recently they _____ (try) to buy a house in the country, but they _____ (not manage) to sell their apartment yet.

5. Jill and Andy _____ (argue) a lot recently because Jill's always going out with her friends.

6. I _____ (eat) so much ice cream, I feel sick!

7. The trains _____ (run) late all morning.

8. Cecilia _____ (cry) all day because she failed all the tests.

9. I _____ (sunbathe) all morning, and now I have a sunburn.

## 2 Present Perfect and Past Simple

Look at Junko Tabei's personal history. Complete the questions and answers.

# *Junko Tabei*
**THE FIRST WOMAN TO CLIMB EVEREST**

| Age | |
|---|---|
| 0 | Born in Fukushima, Japan |
| 4 | Started at Fukushima Elementary School |
| 10 | Went mountain climbing for the first time with her school class |
| 22 | Joined an all-male mountaineering club |
| 23 | Graduated from Showa Women's University with a degree in English and American Literature and devoted herself to mountaineering |
| 26 | Got married |
| 30 | Started the first women's climbing club in Japan |
| 32 | Had her first child, a daughter |
| 36 | Climbed Mount Everest and received a medal from the King of Nepal |
| 39 | Had a son |
| 53 | Became the first woman to climb the Seven Summits (the highest mountain in each of the seven continents) |
| 64 | Climbed her 113th mountain |

1. Where **was Junko Tabei born?**
   In _____.

2. Which _____ to?
   **Fukushima Elementary School.**

3. How long _____ climbing?
   Since she _____.

4. What _____ in college?
   _____.

5. How long _____ married?
   _____ over 38 years.

6. What _____ she was 30?
   _____.

7. When _____ Mount Everest?
   _____ 36.

8. Who _____ a medal?
   The _____.

9. How many _____ climbed?
   _____.

10. Has _____ exciting life?
    _____.

## Simple or continuous?

▶▶▶ **Grammar Reference 1.2 Student Book pp. 136–137**

### 3 Spiderboy

1 Read about Scott Cory and <u>underline</u> the correct verb forms.

# Spiderboy

JENNIFER CORY (1) *stands* / *is standing* in Yosemite National Park, California, looking through a powerful telescope. She looks like a bird-watcher, but she (2) *actually watches* / *is actually watching* her 14-year-old son, Scott, who (3) *climbs* / *is climbing* the face of a 2,900-foot mountain. He (4) *has climbed* / *has been climbing* all morning, and he (5) *has nearly reached* / *has nearly been reaching* the top.

Scott Cory is the American schoolboy rock-climbing sensation. He (6) *has already climbed* / *has already been climbing* some of the highest, most dangerous rock faces in the world. He (7) *started climbing* / *was starting climbing* when he was seven, and he (8) *broke* / *was breaking* his first record when he was 11. He (9) *became* / *was becoming* the youngest person to climb the famous El Capitan mountain in one day. He (10) *has been named* / *has been being named* "Spiderboy" by the press.

Scott (11) *trains* / *is training* at least five hours a day, four days a week. He (12) *has prepared* / *has been preparing* for months for his latest challenge. Next month he (13) *will climb* / *will be climbing* La Esfinge mountain in Peru. Steve Schneider, his fellow rock climber, says, "I (14) *haven't seen* / *haven't been seeing* any other kids do what he does."

2 **CD 5** Complete the e-mail with the verbs in the box in the correct form.

| do (× 2) | arrive | choose | stay | go | become |
|----------|--------|--------|------|------|--------|
| train | call | be | not be | look | make |
| take | prepare | not enjoy | sound | get | |

Dear Mom and Dad,

Lots of love from sunny Peru! I (1) **'m doing** fine so far, and Steve (2) _____ good care of me as usual. We (3) _____ at Lima airport last night. I (4) _____ the flight much. It was very long!

Lima is very hot and crowded, but we (5) _____ only _____ here for one more night. Tomorrow we (6) _____ to La Esfinge to take a look. Steve says that out of all the mountains here, he (7) _____ the hardest climb for us! The route (8) _____ "Welcome to the Slabs of Koricancha." Funny name, eh?

I think this climb (9) _____ harder than anything I (10) _____ in my life. The high altitude (11) _____ it difficult to breathe, and there (12) _____ many hand and foot holds because the rock face is so smooth. But I (13) _____ forward to it. It (14) _____ like a lot of fun!

I (15) _____ so hard recently, and I think I (16) _____ enough for this climb. So please don't worry about me. If we (17) _____ to the top, we (18) _____ the first Americans to do it!

Wish me luck, and thanks for everything, Mom and Dad.

Lots of love!

# Passive

▶▶ **Grammar Reference 1.2 Student Book p. 137**

## 4 Present Perfect passive

**1** Rewrite the sentences using the passive. Omit the subject of the active sentence.

1. The mail carrier has already delivered the mail.

   *The mail has already been delivered.*

2. Have the workmen repaired the street lights yet?

   _____?

3. The government has just passed some new immigration laws.

   _____.

4. The local government hasn't built any new homes for 20 years.

   _____.

5. Nobody has watered the plants.

   _____.

**2** Rewrite the newspaper headlines using the Present Perfect passive.

1. **Rat Alert at Five-star Hotel**

   *Rats have been found in a five-star hotel.*

2. **Dramatic Rescue of Yachtsman in Pacific**

   _____

3. **Theft of Valuable Jewels from Museum**

   _____

4. **Missing Boy Alive**

   _____

5. **Huge Pay Raise for Congressmen**

   _____

6. **Monsoon Kills 260 in India**

   _____

7. **Ancient Tomb Discovery in Egypt**

   _____

8. **Ferrari Shock – 2,000 Laid Off**

   _____

## 5 *have something done*

 **1** Look at the difference in meaning between these three sentences:

> *I've fixed* my bicycle. = I fixed it myself.
>
> *My bicycle has been fixed.* = Someone fixed it. It is not important to know who did it.
>
> *I've had* my bicycle *fixed*. = I arranged/paid for someone to fix it for me. (*have* + object + past participle)

**2** *Have something done* is used to talk about services that you ask someone else to do.

> *I'm going to have my hair cut.*

**1** Rewrite the sentences using *have something done*.

1. John's kitchen is being decorated.

   John's *having the kitchen decorated.*

2. My sister wants someone to pierce her ears.

   My sister wants to _____.

3. My eyes are going to be tested.

   I'm going to _____.

4. Mr. and Mrs. Turner's car has been repaired.

   Mr. and Mrs. Turner _____.

5. Our television hasn't been fixed yet.

   We haven't _____.

**2** It's Melanie and Ken's wedding day. Look at the notes and write sentences about what they have had done or are having done.

*She's had her wedding dress made.*
*He ...*
*They ...*

> RECENTLY — wedding dress made (M)
>   — the invitations printed (M & K)
>   — the cake decorated (M & K)
>
> YESTERDAY — flowers delivered (M & K)
>   — hair cut (K)
>
> TODAY — hair done (M)
>   — cake delivered (M & K)
>
> NEXT WEEK — photos developed (K)
>   — wedding dress dry-cleaned (M)

# Vocabulary

## 6 *make* or *do*?

**1** Complete the conversations with *make* or *do* in the correct form.

1. **A** How many party invitations do we need?

   **B** Mmm. Let me see. Fifty. That'll (1) **do** .

2. **A** Can't you (2) _____ more of an effort with your schoolwork, Joe?

   **B** Well, I'm (3) _____ my best, Dad!

3. **A** What have you bought all that old furniture for?

   **B** I'm going to renovate and sell it! I think I'll (4) _____ a nice profit on it.

   **A** Is this what you're going to (5) _____ for a living now? What happened to your job at the bank?

   **B** It was boring. And then they asked me to work overtime! I'm not working on Saturday mornings, no way.

   **A** But it was a good job! You could've (6) _____ well there.

   **B** Well, I didn't like the manager much. I don't think I (7) _____ a very good impression on him.

   **A** Well, I'm not surprised! You never (8) _____ it to work on time.

   **B** Anyway, you should have seen his face when I told him I was leaving. It (9) _____ my day!

   **A** Oh, that (10) _____ it! I can (11) _____ without all your get-rich-quick schemes! I'm going to look for another boyfriend!

*"The food's pretty bad here, but we make up for it with exceptionally large portions."*

**2** Complete the sentences with the expressions in the box in the correct form.

| | |
|---|---|
| make up for sth | make off with sth |
| ~~make it big~~ | make sth of sb |
| do without sb | could do with sth |
| make it to sth in time | |

1. Wow! Look at your name in lights outside the theater! You've really **made it big** !

2. Thank you so much for helping me! I couldn't _____.

3. **A** What happened to my sandwich?

   **B** I'm afraid the dog grabbed it and _____! Sorry.

4. Flowers and chocolates? I know you're trying to _____ forgetting my birthday, but you'll have to try harder than that.

5. I'm really hungry. I _____ a big steak and fries right now.

6. Cathy acts really strangely sometimes. I don't know what to _____.

7. I'm late! I'll never _____ to the station _____!

## 7 Travel and transportation

**1** Put a check (✓) next to the verbs which go with each form of transportation.

| | car | bus | bike | train | plane | ship/ferry |
|---|---|---|---|---|---|---|
| get into/out of | ✓ | | | | | |
| get on/off | | | | | | |
| ride | | | | | | |
| drive | | | | | | |
| catch | | | | | | |
| miss | | | | | | |
| board | | | | | | |
| park | | | | | | |
| take off | | | | | | |
| land | | | | | | |

**2** Complete the chart below with the nouns in the box. Some can go into more than one column.

| runway | platform | seat belt |
|---|---|---|
| crash helmet | harbor | caboose |
| traffic lights | life jacket | conductor |
| service station | round-trip ticket | luggage cart |
| tires | track | horn |
| cargo | port | one-way street |
| check-in desk | traffic jam | timetable |
| carry-on luggage | Customs | deck |
| tunnel | porter | cabin |
| aisle seat | charter flight | bicycle lane |

| car | bus | bike |
|---|---|---|
| | | |

| train | plane | ship/ferry |
|---|---|---|
| | runway | |

# Prepositions

## 8 Prepositions of movement

Complete the text with the prepositions from the box. Use each preposition at least once.

| across | away | on | onto |
|---|---|---|---|
| along | in | up | into |
| back | out of | over | through |
| past | to | toward | at |

# Mark's trip across town

Mark swiped his credit card (1) **_through_** the card reader. He threw his groceries (2) _____ plastic bags, raced (3) _____ the supermarket, and ran (4) _____ the bus stop. His wife, Jane, was flying (5) _____ today from a long business trip, and it was her birthday. He had exactly two hours to put a birthday cake (6) _____ the oven, pull the finished cake (7) _____ the oven, and take a taxi (8) _____ town to meet his wife at the airport. Mark hurried (9) _____ the sidewalk and got (10) _____ the bus stop just as a bus pulled (11) _____ to the curb. Unfortunately, at that moment, one of his plastic grocery bags broke and fell (12) _____ the ground. Eggs, flour, and cake mix spilled all (13) _____ the sidewalk. Luckily nothing was broken. Mark stuffed everything back (14) _____ the other bag as the bus drove (15) _____ without him. It took Mark 30 minutes to walk (16) _____ his apartment building and another hour to make the cake and spread frosting (17) _____ it. Now he was really late! His wife's flight was arriving (18) _____ the airport in 30 minutes. He left the apartment and jumped (19) _____ the nearest taxi, shouting, "Kennedy Airport, quickly, please!" Although the traffic was bad, the driver found an open lane, and the taxi sped (20) _____ the other cars. They reached the airport just as Jane was walking (21) _____ the exit doors with her suitcases.

"Happy birthday, honey!" said Mark.

"Birthday?" said Jane. "Today's Friday. My birthday is on Saturday!"

# Pronunciation

## 9 Word stress

**1** **CD 6** Mark the stressed syllables in the words below. Then practice saying them.

1. explore        exploration
2. Japan        Japanese
3. contribute      contribution
4. industry       industrial
5. economy     economics
6. politics       politician

**2** What is the stress pattern of the words in Exercise 1? Write the words in the correct column in the chart below.

| • ● | • ● • |
|---|---|
| explore | |
| ● • • | • • ● |
| | |
| • • ● • | • ● • • |
| exploration | |

**3** **CD 7** Write the words from the box below in the correct column in the chart above. Listen and check.

| | |
|---|---|
| discovery | develop |
| backpacker | information |
| calculate | abroad |
| destruction | kilometer |
| unique | destroy |
| unspoiled | Vietnam |
| pollution | environment |
| paradise | European |
| destination | diarrhea |
| inhabitant | illegal |

# Listening

## 10 A vacation nightmare

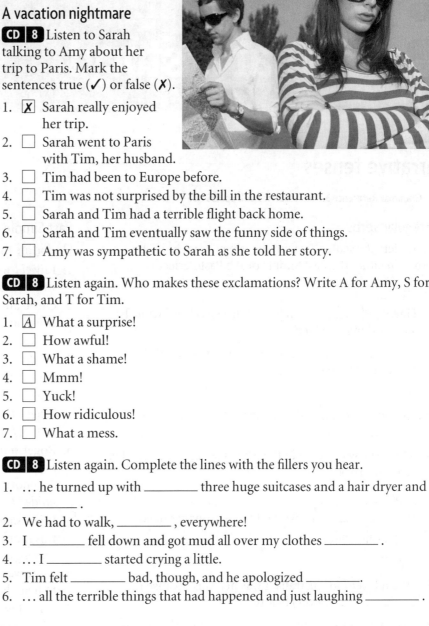

**1** **CD 8** Listen to Sarah talking to Amy about her trip to Paris. Mark the sentences true (✓) or false (✗).

1. ☒ Sarah really enjoyed her trip.
2. ☐ Sarah went to Paris with Tim, her husband.
3. ☐ Tim had been to Europe before.
4. ☐ Tim was not surprised by the bill in the restaurant.
5. ☐ Sarah and Tim had a terrible flight back home.
6. ☐ Sarah and Tim eventually saw the funny side of things.
7. ☐ Amy was sympathetic to Sarah as she told her story.

**2** **CD 8** Listen again. Who makes these exclamations? Write A for Amy, S for Sarah, and T for Tim.

1. ☐A What a surprise!
2. ☐ How awful!
3. ☐ What a shame!
4. ☐ Mmm!
5. ☐ Yuck!
6. ☐ How ridiculous!
7. ☐ What a mess.

**3** **CD 8** Listen again. Complete the lines with the fillers you hear.

1. … he turned up with _____ three huge suitcases and a hair dryer and _____ .
2. We had to walk, _____ , everywhere!
3. I _____ fell down and got mud all over my clothes _____ .
4. … I _____ started crying a little.
5. Tim felt _____ bad, though, and he apologized _____ .
6. … all the terrible things that had happened and just laughing _____ .

# 3 What a story!

**Grammar:** Narrative tenses
**Vocabulary:** The world of literature
**Pronunciation:** Diphthongs

## Narrative tenses

▶▶ **Grammar Reference 3.1–3.5 Student Book pp. 138–139**

### 1 Irregular verbs

**1** Complete the sentences with the irregular verbs in the boxes in either the Past Simple or the Past Perfect.

> fall ☐

1. Harry _fell_____ in love with a Greek girl while he was working in Athens.
2. He _____ in love before, but this was different. He wanted to marry her.

> tear ☐

3. Douglas saw Camilla's coat and asked how she _____ it.
4. While she was hiking in the Alps, she _____ her coat on a rock.

> cost ☐

5. It _____ an awful lot to have our car fixed.
6. Ted told me his new car _____ a fortune.

> fly ☐

7. When I went to Australia, I was nervous because I _____ (never) before.
8. The plane took off and _____ into the clouds.

> catch ☐

9. Suzy wondered how she _____ a cold in the middle of her summer vacation.
10. She _____ a taxi outside the restaurant and went back to her hotel.

> be ☐

11. Talks _____ held in Washington last week to discuss global warming.
12. When the politicians left the talks, no decisions _____ reached.

**2** Put a check (✓) next to the verbs in Exercise 1 which have the same form for the Past Simple and the past participle.

### 2 Past Simple or Past Continuous?

Underline the correct form.

1. I *lived* / *was living* in Tampa when I *met* / *was meeting* my husband.
2. Our team *played* / *was playing* really well and we *won* / *were winning* at halftime, but in the end we *lost* / *were losing* 83–82.
3. I *didn't think* / *wasn't thinking* of having a birthday party, but now I'm glad I *had* / *was having* one.
4. I'm so tired. The baby next door *was coughing* / *coughed* all night long, and we *weren't getting* / *didn't get* any sleep.
5. Roger *sunbathed* / *was sunbathing* by the hotel pool when he *heard* / *was hearing* a strange sound. An enormous insect *appeared* / *was appearing* and *landed* / *was landing* on his leg.
6. It *was snowing* / *snowed* when I *got up* / *was getting up* this morning. The children next door *made* / *were making* a snowman, so I quickly *put* / *was putting* on some warm clothes and *rushed* / *was rushing* outside to help them.
7. Daniel *was playing* / *played* happily in the snow when his big brother *hit* / *was hitting* him and *made* / *was making* him cry.

*"The kids just played quietly all night, like kids do."*

## 3 Which narrative tense?

Complete the article with the verbs in the box.

| Past Simple | | Past Continuous | Past Perfect Simple | Past Perfect Continuous | Present Perfect |
|---|---|---|---|---|---|
| called | said | was recovering | had been knocked | had been surfing | has been |
| felt | shouted | was standing | had hit | ~~had been swimming~~ | have been |
| had to | swam | was trying | had just finished | | |
| heard | was | were getting | had moved | | |
| managed | wasn't | | had taken | | |
| pulled | went back in | | | | |
| reached | | | | | |

# The blind sea hero

## Sightless swimmer saves a surfer

David Hurst (1) **had been swimming** in the sea off the coast near his house in Malibu, California and (2) _____ on the beach when he thought he (3) _____ cries for help.

Despite being totally blind, Mr. Hurst (4) _____ the sea to rescue the person in trouble.

"I (5) _____ just in the right place at the right time to help somebody," the 53-year-old (6) _____ yesterday.

Mr. Hurst, who (7) _____ blind for 23 years, (8) _____ to reach Patrick Black by using the drowning man's cries to guide him. Mr. Black (9) _____ but (10) _____ off his surfboard by a huge wave and (11) _____ his head on a rock. Mr. Hurst (12) _____ through the waves to find him, then (13) _____ Mr. Black and his surfboard back to shore.

Mr. Hurst explained, "I (14) _____ drying myself, when someone (15) _____ 'Help!' I (16) _____ back to him to keep on shouting. I (17) _____ think about the direction of the wind, too. While I (18) _____ to find him, the wind and the waves (19) _____ stronger and stronger. But I just kept going until I finally (20) _____ him and got him back to the shore. It (21) _____ a long time to fight through the high waves, and we (22) _____ completely exhausted." Last night Mr. Black (23) _____ in the hospital from shock and a broken arm.

What was even more remarkable was that Mr. Hurst (24) _____ familiar with the coastline. He and his wife (25) _____ to Malibu only two weeks before.

"Fortunately, I (26) _____ a good swimmer all my life," he said.

## 4 Time expressions

**1** Match the lines and time expressions. Use each expression only once.

| | | | |
|---|---|---|---|
| 1. **e** I've been working in the same bank | | a. | ten years ago. |
| 2. ☐ I started this job | | b. | before my first poem was published. |
| 3. ☐ I didn't want to get married | | | |
| 4. ☐ I had had two children | | c. | by the time I was 40. |
| 5. ☐ I'd been writing poetry for many years | | d. | until I was 30. |
| | | e. | for years. |
| 6. ☐ I didn't stay in that job | | f. | since six o'clock. |
| 7. ☐ I've been waiting here | | g. | until I arrived. |
| 8. ☐ They didn't start ordering the meal | | h. | when he finally arrived. |
| 9. ☐ The train pulled out of the station | | i. | for long. |
| 10. ☐ I'd been waiting over an hour | | j. | a minute ago. |
| 11. ☐ I haven't been feeling well | | k. | until it was too late. |
| 12. ☐ They got on the plane | | l. | until late. |
| 13. ☐ I'd never seen him | | m. | lately. |
| 14. ☐ I was watching TV | | n. | at the last minute. |
| 15. ☐ He didn't hear the attacker | | o. | before. |

**2** Complete the sentences using past tenses only and the prompts in parentheses.

1. Two years ago, _while I was working in Paris, my grandfather died._
   (while / I / work / in Paris / my grandfather / die)

2. As soon as I _____.
   (feed / the cat / I / do / my homework)

3. First I _____.
   (take / a shower / then / I / get dressed)

4. Since I was a child I _____.
   (always / want / visit / Africa / and / I / finally / go / last year)

5. As he _____.
   (mail / the letter / he / realize / he / not put / a stamp)

6. By the time he'd _____.
   (finish / speak / most of the audience / fall asleep)

7. Once I'd _____.
   (tell / him / the truth / I / feel better)

8. Until I _____.
   (find / an apartment / I / stay with / friends / for months)

# Past passives

## 5 Active to passive

Put each sentence into the passive. Omit the subject of the active sentence.

1. Someone stole my bike last night.
   My bike _was stolen last night._____

2. Archaeologists discovered a Roman temple underneath the new building.
   A Roman temple _____
   _____
   _____.

3. They held the races indoors because it was raining.
   The races _____
   _____.

4. Someone had booked the restaurant for a private party on Saturday.
   The restaurant _____
   _____
   _____.

5. The plumber was repairing the dishwasher, so I couldn't leave the house.
   The dishwasher _____
   _____.

6. When we returned to our hotel room, they still hadn't cleaned it.
   Our hotel room _____
   _____
   _____.

7. The chef hadn't cooked the fish long enough.
   The fish _____
   _____.

8. Workmen were putting up new traffic lights at the intersection.
   New traffic lights _____
   _____.

# Review of active and passive

## 6 Movie review

**CD 9** Read the review and complete it with the verbs in the boxes in the correct form, active or passive.

# A short story made long

***Where the Wild Things Are* is good, but the book is better,**

says Erin Lee

..........................

| build | base | ~~show~~ | regard | film | use |
|---|---|---|---|---|---|

Don't get me wrong. I liked *Where the Wild Things Are*. When the movie (1) **was shown** in the theaters last week, kids and their parents liked it, too. But the children's book the movie (2) _____ on is the one that (3) _____ as a classic.

The most striking thing about the movie was the way it looked. Very little computer animation (4) _____. Instead, the filmmakers (5) _____ beautiful sets and costumes and (6) _____ it all in natural sunlight.

| eat | become | play | ignore | punish | learn |
|---|---|---|---|---|---|

The movie is all about Max, a smart, lonely boy who (7) _____ by his older sister and her friends. When Max misbehaves and (8) _____ by his mother, he leaves home and sails to a mysterious island full of monsters. At first, Max (9) _____ almost _____ by the monsters. But Max (who (10) _____ brilliantly by the young actor Max Records) quickly (11) _____ their king. Eventually, however, Max (12) _____ that the monsters have the same troubles as the humans he left behind.

| suffer | not | speak | write | give | add | depress | know |
|---|---|---|---|---|---|---|---|

The monsters look adorable but are not so great to listen to. In Maurice Sendak's book, the monsters (13) _____ . In the movie, they (14) _____ voices by famous Hollywood actors like James Gandolfini, who (15) _____ best _____ as the mafia boss in *The Sopranos*. This is very distracting.

Also, because the book is short, additional material (16) _____ to make the movie longer. In the book, the monsters just roar and have fun, but in the movie they (17) _____ from loneliness, social anxiety, and relationship troubles. While the book (18) _____ to entertain children, it seems the movie's goal is to (19) _____ their parents.

# Vocabulary

## 7 The world of literature

The following words are related to prose, poetry, or drama. Put them into the correct columns. Some words can go into more than one column.

nursery rhyme
plot
chapter
critic
director
backstage
best-seller
script
review
character
leading role
novelist
blockbuster
verse
fairy tale
setting
mystery
rehearsal
science fiction
hardcover
performance
thriller
playwright
autobiography
act
full house
paperback

| Poetry | Prose | Drama |
|---|---|---|
| nursery rhyme | | |

# Phrasal verbs

## 8 Type 1 phrasal verbs

 There are four types of phrasal verbs. Types 2 and 3 are on page 34 in Unit 5, and type 4 is on page 46 in Unit 7 of this Workbook.
Type 1 phrasal verbs consist of a verb + particle. There is no object.
They can be both literal and metaphorical.

*She **stood up** and **walked out**.* (literal)

*The bomb **went off**.* (metaphorical)

**1** Match the phrasal verbs in **A** with their definition in **B**.

| A | B |
|---|---|
| 1. [c] shut up | a. have a calmer, more stable life |
| 2. ☐ break up | b. wait a minute |
| 3. ☐ hold on | c. be quiet |
| 4. ☐ speak up | d. begin a trip |
| 5. ☐ set off | e. be happier |
| 6. ☐ stay in | f. not go out, stay at home |
| 7. ☐ settle down | g. talk louder |
| 8. ☐ turn up | h. finally appear |
| 9. ☐ cheer up | i. end a relationship |

**2** Complete the sentences with the phrasal verbs from Exercise 1. Put the verbs in the correct form.

1. Peter hasn't arrived yet. I hope he <u>'ll turn up</u> soon.

2. We have a long trip tomorrow. What time do we have to _____?

3. Why are you so miserable? _____!

4. I don't feel like going out tonight. Should we _____ and order a pizza?

5. Larry was a bit wild at college, but then he got a job, found a wife, _____, and had kids.

6. After three years of going out together, Josh and Lil eventually _____ because Lil didn't want to get married.

7. _____! I'm trying to watch TV and you're all talking.

8. **A** What's Bill's phone number?'
   **B** _____! I'll look it up.

9. _____! We can't hear you in the back!

# Pronunciation

## 9 Diphthongs

> ⚠ Diphthongs are two vowel sounds which run together.
> **bye** /baɪ/ = /a/ + /ɪ/ diphthong /aɪ/
> **boy** /bɔɪ/ = /ɔ/ + /ɪ/ diphthong /ɔɪ/

**1** **CD 10** Match the words in A with a rhyming one in B.

| A | B |
|---|---|
| 1. [d] soy | a. buy |
| 2. [ ] lie | b. shown |
| 3. [ ] pay | c. browned |
| 4. [ ] round | d. toy |
| 5. [ ] phone | e. hey |

**2** **CD 11** Read the poem aloud. Write the number next to the word that rhymes with the one in *italics*.

## sounds and letters don't agree

| | | | |
|---|---|---|---|
| **When the English tongue we speak,** | | | |
| **Why does (1) *break* not rhyme with (2) *weak*?** | [2] cheek | [1] cake | |
| **Won't you tell me why it's true** | | | |
| **We say (3) *sew*, but also (4) *few*?** | [ ] flu | [ ] flow | |
| **And the maker of a verse** | | | |
| **Cannot rhyme his (5) *horse* with (6) *worse*?** | [ ] course | [ ] nurse | |
| **(7) *Beard* is not the same as (8) *heard*.** | [ ] bird | [ ] weird | |
| **(9) *Cord* is different from (10) *word*,** | [ ] third | [ ] board | |
| **(11) *Cow* is cow, but (12) *low* is low,** | [ ] dough | [ ] bough | |
| **(13) *Shoe* is never rhymed with (14) *foe*.** | [ ] knew | [ ] show | |
| **Think of (15) *hose* and (16) *dose* and (17) *lose*,** | [ ] cruise | [ ] rose | [ ] gross |
| **And think of (18) *loose* and yet of (19) *choose*,** | [ ] news | [ ] juice | |
| **Think of (20) *comb* and (21) *tomb* and (22) *bomb*,** | [ ] mom | [ ] room | [ ] dome |
| **(23) *Doll* and (24) *roll*** | [ ] fall | [ ] goal | |
| **and (25) *home* and (26) *some*.** | [ ] gum | [ ] Rome | |
| **And since *pay* is rhymed with *say*,** | | | |
| **Why not (27) *paid* with (28) *said*, I pray?** | [ ] shade | [ ] red | |
| **Think of (29) *blood* and (30) *food* and (31) *good*;** | [ ] would | [ ] rude | [ ] mud |
| **Rhyme them all I wish I could.** | | | |
| **Why is it (32) *done*, but (33) *gone* and (34) *lone*?** | [ ] own | [ ] lawn | [ ] fun |
| **Is there any reason known?** | | | |
| **To sum up, it seems to me** | | | |
| **That sounds and letters don't agree.** | | | |

# Listening

## 10 What an amazing coincidence!

**1** **CD 12** Listen and answer the questions.

1. What was the program that Becky saw?
2. What happened to the young mother and her baby?
3. Where was the father?
4. What did the mother tell her daughter?
5. Where did the daughter move to?
6. Who did she go to have dinner with?
7. Who did she meet?
8. How did her mother feel?
9. What were the amazing coincidences in the story?

**2** **CD 12** Listen again. Put the phrases for giving and responding to news in the order that you hear them.

a [ ] I don't believe it!
b [ ] Apparently …
c [1] Did you see that program about … ?
d [ ] Really?
e [ ] Tell me.
f [ ] Actually …
g [ ] Then what happened?
h [ ] That's amazing!
i [ ] Don't tell me that …
j [ ] You're kidding!

# 4 Nothing but the truth

## Negatives

▶▶ **Grammar Reference 4.2 Student Book p. 140**

### 1 Negative auxiliaries

Complete the sentences with the negative auxiliaries in the box.

| | | | | |
|---|---|---|---|---|
| isn't | aren't | 'm not | hasn't | didn't |
| doesn't | ~~don't~~ | hadn't | won't | haven't |

1. Jackie speaks fluent French, but I _don't_____.
2. We wanted to leave the party, but Fred _____.
3. I've been to Canada, but my parents _____.
4. Fords are made here, but BMWs _____.
5. She was getting better before, but now she _____.
6. I'll be moving to New Orleans, but my girlfriend _____.
7. My daughter's going to the party, but I _____.
8. Jodi likes Indian food, but Andrew _____.
9. Ed thought I'd forgotten our wedding anniversary, but I _____.
10. The kitchen's been decorated, but the bathroom _____.

### 2 _no, not, -n't,_ or _none_?

Complete the sentences with _no, not, -n't,_ or _none_.

1. I'll help you but _not___ tonight.
2. We have _no___ onions left. Sorry.
3. _None_ of us understood the lesson.
4. The teacher was _n't___ very clear.
5. I asked you _____ to make a mess.
6. Why did _____ you do what I asked?
7. How do you manage _____ to put on any weight?
8. Bring Alessia to the party but _____ Ben. He's too loud.
9. There's _____ meat in this dish, so it's suitable for vegetarians.
10. **A** Who likes algebra?
    **B** _____ me.
11. **A** Where's the nearest swimming pool?
    **B** There are _____ around here.
12. She has _____ idea how to enjoy herself.
13. Why have _____ you e-mailed me for so long?
14. I can cook but _____ the way my mother does.
15. **A** Do you work late?
    **B** _____ if I can help it.
16. **A** Where's the coffee?
    **B** There's _____ left.
17. _____ plants can survive without water.
18. I have _____ time for people who are rude.
19. _____ of my friends are rich.
20. **A** Do you like jazz?
    **B** _____ usually.

## 3 Opposite meanings

Rewrite the sentences to give them the opposite meaning. Make any necessary changes using negative forms and antonyms.

1. She's rich. She has lots of money.
   _She's poor. She doesn't have any money at all._

2. I told you to go to work. Why are you in bed?

   _____

   _____

3. Tom was a successful businessman who achieved a lot in his life.

   _____

   _____

4. Our house is difficult to find. Everybody always gets lost.

   _____

   _____

5. We had a wonderful time in Venice. There weren't many people there.

   _____

   _____

6. You should exercise your ankle. Try to move it as much as possible.

   _____

   _____

7. I have to iron my shirt. I'm going out tonight.

   _____

   _____

8. You need to come with me. I won't go on my own.

   _____

   _____

9. I was in a hurry because I needed to go to the store.

   _____

   _____

10. All of the students passed the test, so their teacher was pleased.

    _____

    _____

## 4 I don't think you're right.

1. In English we usually say *I don't think* + affirmative verb:

   *I **don't think** I **know** you.*
   NOT ~~I think I don't know you.~~

   We do the same with *believe*, and *expect*.

   *I **don't expect** we'll meet again.*
   *My parents **didn't believe** I'd pass my exams.*

2. We can also use *seem, expect,* and *want* with the negative + infinitive:

   *She **doesn't** seem **to be** very happy.*
   *I **don't** expect **to get** the job.*
   *They **don't** want me **to go back** there.*
   *I **don't** expect you **to do** that.*

Rewrite the sentences using the verb in parentheses in the negative.

1. You haven't met my wife. (I think)
   _I don't think you've met my wife._

2. This machine isn't working. (This machine seems)

   _____

3. It wasn't going to rain. (I thought)

   _____

4. Their daughter's moving to Germany. They aren't happy. (They want)

   _____

5. I'm surprised to see you here. (I expect)

   _____

6. I wouldn't like snails. (I think)

   _____

7. You probably don't remember me. (I expect)

   _____

8. She didn't pass all her exams. (I believe)

   _____

# Questions

▶▶ **Grammar Reference 4.1 Student Book pp. 139–140**

## 5 Catch me if you can

Read the text about Frank Abagnale and write questions for the answers.

**Frank Abagnale** was a successful con man for five years. Amazingly, he started at 16. Steven Spielberg made the movie *Catch Me If You Can* about him, starring Leonardo DiCaprio and Tom Hanks.

In 1964, Frank ran away to New York, upset because his parents had divorced. He was tall and handsome with prematurely graying hair, so he decided to pretend he was 26 to get a job.

His first scam was to forge bank checks. When the bank found out, he had already collected $40,000. He had to change his identity, so he became Frank Williams, a Pan Am Airways pilot. He conned Pan Am into giving him a pilot's uniform, and he faked an ID card. For two years he traveled around the world for free with paid hotel expenses! But after he told his secret to his flight attendant girlfriend, she called the police, and he had to disappear again.

Next he became a lawyer. He forged a Harvard law degree and then studied to pass the bar exam! He was also a hospital doctor and a university professor. He taught sociology, and apparently his classes were very popular. Each time he had to move on before the police caught up with him.

He was eventually arrested in France in 1969 and sent to prison for five years.

Since then, he has worked as a financial fraud consultant!

1. <u>How long was Frank Abagnale a con man for</u>_____?
   Five years.

2. _____?
   Steven Spielberg.

3. _____ to New York?
   Sixteen.

4. _____?
   Because he was upset about his parents' divorce.

5. _____?
   He was tall and handsome with graying hair.

6. _____?
   Forging bank checks.

7. _____?
   $40,000.

8. _____?
   Two years.

9. _____?
   His girlfriend.

10. _____?
    A lawyer.

11. _____?
    Sociology.

12. _____?
    In 1969.

13. _____?
    Five years.

14. _____ since then?
    Working as a financial fraud consultant.

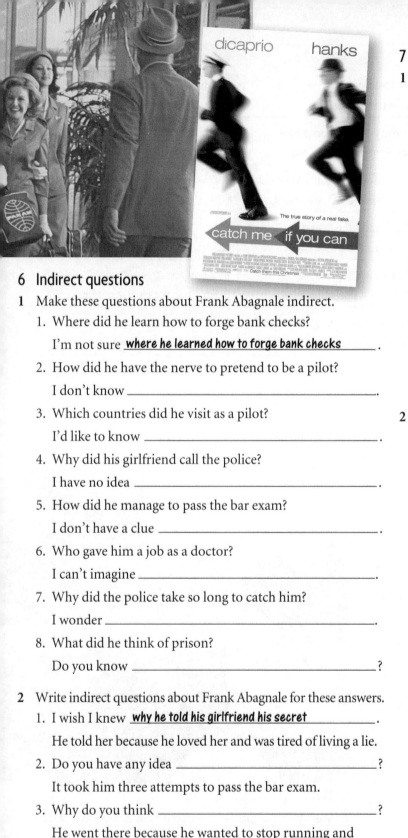

dicaprio    hanks

The true story of a real fake.

catch me    if you can

Catch them this Christmas

## 6 Indirect questions

**1** Make these questions about Frank Abagnale indirect.

1. Where did he learn how to forge bank checks?

   I'm not sure _where he learned how to forge bank checks_ .

2. How did he have the nerve to pretend to be a pilot?

   I don't know _____.

3. Which countries did he visit as a pilot?

   I'd like to know _____.

4. Why did his girlfriend call the police?

   I have no idea _____.

5. How did he manage to pass the bar exam?

   I don't have a clue _____.

6. Who gave him a job as a doctor?

   I can't imagine _____.

7. Why did the police take so long to catch him?

   I wonder _____.

8. What did he think of prison?

   Do you know _____?

**2** Write indirect questions about Frank Abagnale for these answers.

1. I wish I knew _why he told his girlfriend his secret_ .

   He told her because he loved her and was tired of living a lie.

2. Do you have any idea _____?

   It took him three attempts to pass the bar exam.

3. Why do you think _____?

   He went there because he wanted to stop running and settle down in one place.

4. Can you tell me _____?

   He spent five years in prison.

5. Do you know _____?

   He says he is sorry for what he did and has spent the rest of his life being a model citizen.

## 7 Questions and prepositions

**1** Complete the questions with the prepositions in the box. Use each preposition only once.

| in | of | by | with | to | from | at | about | ~~for~~ | on |
|----|----|----|------|----|------|----|-------|--------|----|

1. What is your hometown famous _for_ ?

2. Who was that book written _____?

3. Who does this dictionary belong _____?

4. What are you looking _____?

5. What did you spend all your money _____?

6. What sort of books are you interested _____?

7. What are you talking _____?

8. What are you so afraid _____?

9. **A** You got a postcard.

   **B** Oh. Who is it _____?

10. Who are you angry _____? James or me?

**2** Write a short question with a preposition in reply to these sentences.

1. **A** I went to a movie last night.
   **B** _Who with?_

2. **A** I'm very angry with you.
   **B** _____?

3. **A** We're going away for the weekend.
   **B** _____?

4. **A** I'm very worried.
   **B** _____?

5. **A** I'm going to Morocco.
   **B** _____? Two weeks? A month?

6. **A** I bought a present today.
   **B** _____ ? Your wife?

7. **A** Have you heard? Jane got engaged.
   **B** _____?

8. **A** Can you cut this article out for me?
   **B** _____? I don't have any scissors.

## 8 Negative questions

▶▶ Grammar Reference 4.2
Student Book p. 140

Match a question in **A** with
a line in **B** that follows it.

| A | | B |
|---|---|---|
| 1. **b** Are you ready yet? | | a. What have you been doing all this time? |
| 2. ☐ Aren't you ready yet? | | b. It's time to go. |
| 3. ☐ Don't you want me to help you? | | c. I thought you did. |
| 4. ☐ Do you want me to help you? | | d. I will if you want. |
| 5. ☐ Aren't you a member of the tennis club? | | e. I'm sure I've seen you there. |
| 6. ☐ Are you a member of the tennis club? | | f. If you are, we could meet there. |
| 7. ☐ Don't you know the answer? | | g. I can't figure it out. |
| 8. ☐ Do you know the answer? | | h. I'm surprised at you! |
| 9. ☐ Don't you think it's beautiful? | | i. Surely you agree with me! |
| 10. ☐ Do you think it's beautiful? | | j. I'm asking because I'm not sure. |
| 11. ☐ Didn't I tell you I'm going out tonight? | | k. I can't remember now. |
| 12. ☐ Did I tell you I'm going out tonight? | | l. I thought I had. Sorry. |

## 9 *Can you keep a secret?*

**CD 13** Complete the questions in the conversation.
Sometimes there is more than one answer.

**A** I went to a party last night.

**B** Did you? (1) **Whose** _____?

**A** Belinda's. You know, my friend from work.

**B** Oh, yes. What (2) _____?

**A** It was really good. I talked with various people.

**B** (3) _____?

**A** Well, I talked for a long time to Vicky, you know, from school.

**B** Of course. Brainy Vicky. (4) _____?

**A** She's fine. Got a good job. But actually, she's not very happy right now.

**B** (5) _____?

**A** I don't know if I can tell you. Look, you can keep a secret, (6) _____?

**B** Of course I can. So, what (7) _____?

**A** She's having a terrible time with her boyfriend, Sam.

**B** (8) _____?

**A** You remember. He was a year ahead of us in school.

**B** (9) _____?

**A** You know. Tall. Dark curly hair. Nice smile.

**B** Oh, yes, I remember now. (10) _____ use to wear glasses?

**A** That's right. But he doesn't anymore. Anyway, they had been talking about getting married and everything, when suddenly he turned all funny and cold toward her.

**B** (11) _____?

**A** Well, turns out that he's been seeing another girl as well lately!

**B** No! (12) _____?

**A** You'll never guess! Your neighbor, Tessa!

**B** Not Tessa! I can't believe it! (13) _____ Vicky _____ now?

**A** She's going to try to forgive him. Apparently, he's very sorry. But don't tell anyone.

# Vocabulary

## 10 Antonyms and synonyms

**1** For the words in **A**, write their opposites in **B**, using prefixes.

| A<br>Adjectives | B | C |
|---|---|---|
| a. truthful | untruthful | dishonest |
| b. real | | |
| c. complete | | |
| d. plausible | | |
| e. probable | | |
| f. pleased | | |
| g. normal | | |
| h. professional | | |
| i. important | | |
| **Nouns** | | |
| j. honesty | | |
| k. reality | | |
| l. belief | | |
| **Verbs** | | |
| m. appear | | |
| n. understand | | |
| o. trust | | |
| p. cover | | |

**2** In column **C** in the chart above, write synonyms for the words in **B** using the words in the box below.

| | |
|---|---|
| fake | confuse |
| dishonest | reveal |
| deceit | unbelievable |
| fantasy | vanish |
| partial | annoyed |
| bizarre | amateur |
| unlikely | trivial |
| incredulity | suspect |

# Prepositions

## 11 Verb + preposition

Many verbs are followed by prepositions. Complete the sentences with the correct prepositions.

1. I agree **with** every word you say.
2. I applied _____ the job, but I didn't get it.
3. What are you all laughing _____? What's the joke?
4. He died _____ a heart attack.
5. She's suffering badly _____ sunburn.
6. Do you believe _____ magic?
7. I didn't realize that Marina was married _____ George.
8. Did you succeed _____ convincing your father you were telling the truth?
9. Compared _____ you, I'm not very intelligent at all!
10. We've complained _____ our teacher _____ the amount of homework we get.
11. Stop laughing _____ me. It isn't funny!
12. I've completely fallen _____ love _____ you.
13. Who are you going to vote _____ in the next election?
14. Tom Hanks has appeared _____ more than 15 major movies.

# Listening

## 12 It's a conspiracy!

**1** **CD 14** Listen to the radio program about the death of Marilyn Monroe. Mark the sentences true (✓) or false (✗).

1. ☐ Adam Phillips is a radio host.
2. ☐ Adam Phillips did not know Marilyn Monroe personally.
3. ☐ Marilyn Monroe was married to Frank Sinatra.
4. ☐ Marilyn Monroe knew the President.
5. ☐ There are many conspiracy theories about the death of Marilyn Monroe.
6. ☐ The police assumed she took too many sleeping pills.
7. ☐ Her psychiatrist said he saw Bobby Kennedy visit her house.
8. ☐ Adam Phillips believes that the Kennedy family had Marilyn Monroe killed.
9. ☐ Joe DiMaggio frequently talked about his suspicions of the Kennedys.

**2** **CD 14** Listen again. Complete the lines with the polite expressions you hear.

1. _____ start by telling us why Marilyn was so famous?
2. _____ give a few examples of that.
3. _____ telling us about some of those theories?
4. _____ give a little background about her death?
5. _____ where she turned up a year later?
6. Oh, _____ , but _____ , we need to take a short break.

# Pronunciation

## 13 Intonation in question tags

> ❗ **CD 15** In question tags the intonation either falls ⟶ or rises ⟶ .
>
> 1 ⟶ Falling intonation means that the sentence is more like a statement = "I'm sure I'm right. Can you just confirm this for me?"
>
> *It's really warm again today, isn't it?*
> *You've lost the car keys again, haven't you?*
>
> 2 ⟶ Rising intonation means that the sentence is more like a real question = "I'm not sure if I'm right about this. Correct me if I'm wrong."
>
> *You've been invited to Jane's party, haven't you?*
> *Ted didn't fail his driver's test again, did he?*
>
> Both patterns are very common in spoken English because they invite other people to join in the conversation.

**1** **CD 16** Write the question tags for the statements. Mark whether it falls or rises.

1. You're angry with me, **aren't you** ⟶ ?
2. Last night was such a hot night, _____ ?
3. Anthony's late again, _____ ?
4. It's cold for this time of year, _____ ?
5. I'm just terrible at telling jokes, _____ ?
6. You haven't seen my pen anywhere, _____ ?
7. By the end of the movie we were all in tears, _____ ?
8. You wouldn't have change for a ten-dollar bill, _____ ?

**2** **CD 17** Write a sentence and a question tag for these situations. Mark whether the intonation falls or rises.

1. You're coming out of a restaurant where you have just had a really terrible meal with a friend.

   That **meal was really terrible, wasn't it** ⟶ ?

2. You can't believe that your sister has borrowed your new coat again.

   You _____ ?

3. You need a neighbor to water your plants while you're away.

   You _____ ?

4. You think that Vanessa is going on a business trip to Oslo next week, but you're not sure.

   Vanessa, you _____ ?

# 5 An eye to the future

**Grammar:** Future forms
**Vocabulary:** *take* or *put*?
**Pronunciation:** Sounds and spelling

## Future forms

▶▶ **Grammar Reference 5.1–5.8 Student Book pp. 140–142**

### 1 Question tags

Match a sentence in **A** with a question tag in **B**.

| A | | B |
|---|---|---|
| 1. | [j] You're going to work harder from now on, | a. will we? |
| 2. | ☐ I'll see you on Sunday, | b. doesn't it? |
| 3. | ☐ Kate's leaving soon, | c. won't we? |
| 4. | ☐ You'll call when you get there, | d. are you? |
| 5. | ☐ Our plane takes off at 4 P.M., | e. won't I? |
| 6. | ☐ The decorators will have finished by next week, | f. isn't she? |
| 7. | ☐ You aren't getting married next month, | g. won't you? |
| 8. | ☐ We won't need tickets to get in, | h. won't they? |
| 9. | ☐ We'll be millionaires one day, | i. will he? |
| 10. | ☐ Max won't be coming, | j. aren't you? |

I THINK I'LL WAIT FOR IT TO COOL DOWN A BIT!

### 2 *will* or *going to*?

Complete the conversations with *will* or *going to* in the correct form. Sometimes there is more than one answer.

1. **A** I **'m going to** make myself a sandwich. Do you want one?

   **B** No thanks. I _____ have something later.

2. **A** Marco and Lia _____ Florida on vacation this year.

   **B** How wonderful! The boys _____ love it, especially Disney World.

3. **A** Bye, Mom. I _____ meet Tom and Mel. I _____ be back at about ten o'clock.

   **B** OK, but don't be late again or I _____ be really annoyed.

4. **A** Linda _____ be furious when she finds out I crashed the car.

   **B** She _____ understand if you explain that it wasn't your fault.

5. **A** I _____ (not) work today. I feel awful.

   **B** Don't worry, I _____ call your boss and tell her you're sick.

6. **A** I'm tired. I think I _____ go to bed.

   **B** I _____ watch the news, then I _____ join you.

7. **A** My boss has told me I _____ be promoted.

   **B** Congratulations! We _____ have to celebrate!

8. **A** Mr. Smith, now that you've won the lottery you _____ be the fifth-richest man in the country. How do you feel about that?

   **B** I _____ tell you next week. I'm too shocked right now!

## 3 What does Ling say?

Write what Ling actually says in these situations. Use a future form.

1. She sees some very black clouds in the sky.

   Ling: **"It's going to rain."** _____

2. Her brother has just reminded her that it is her grandfather's birthday soon.

   Ling: "I _____."

3. She has decided to look for a new job.

   Ling: "I _____."

4. She's made an appointment to see the doctor next Tuesday.

   Ling: "I _____."

5. She predicts a win for her team, the Dallas Cowboys, on Sunday.

   Ling: "I think _____."

6. She's stuck in a traffic jam. She's late for a movie. She calls her friend.

   Ling: "I'm sorry. _____."

7. Her sister is pregnant. The baby is due next March.

   Ling: "My sister _____."

8. Her train ticket for tomorrow says: Departure 2:30 P.M.

   Ling: "My train _____."

9. She can see herself skiing in Canada next week at this time.

   Ling: "This time next week _____."

10. She predicts snow there.

    Ling: "I think it _____."

## 4 Future Continuous or Future Perfect?

Tracey is a student right now. Look at her plans for things she thinks she will have done or she will be doing by the time she's 40. Write what she thinks using either the Future Continuous or Future Perfect.

1. move to Los Angeles
2. work hard in the movie industry
3. live in a big house
4. act in a Hollywood movie
5. make at least $1 million a year
6. hang out with lots of famous friends
7. swim in the ocean every day
8. get very fit
9. marry a nice man
10. have two children

By the time I'm 40 ...

1. **I'll have moved to Los Angeles.** _____
2. **I'll be working hard in the movie industry.** _____
3. _____
4. _____
5. _____
6. _____
7. _____
8. _____
9. _____
10. _____

## 5 Slugger and singer in the city

Underline the appropriate future form.

# Slugger and singer in the city

*Star Report* meets up with **Zoe Fox** and **Chris Green** in New York in the spring on their first wedding anniversary.

**STAR REPORT** Hello, Zoe and Chris. What are you planning to do while you are in New York?

**Zoe** We (1) *'re going to celebrate* / *celebrate* the fact that we're back together again. And, of course, we (2) *'ll have bought* / *'ll be buying* lots of presents for our family!

**STAR REPORT** Yes, you both split up briefly last year. What are your plans for the coming year?

**Zoe** The split was my fault. I was spending too much time on tour, and Chris had no one to take care of him at home. I (3) *'ll never leave* / *'ll never be leaving* him again for such a long time.

**Chris** Yes, it was only a temporary split. It (4) *won't happen* / *isn't happening* again. We love each other, and we (5) *'ll be married* / *'ll have been married* until the end of our days.

**STAR REPORT** Zoe, what (6) *will you be doing* / *will you have done* now that you've finished your touring days?

**Zoe** Well, I (7) *'m going to record* / *'ll record* a new album, since I've just signed a new record deal.

**STAR REPORT** Chris, you're a home-run hitting baseball star at the height of your popularity. What (8) *will you be trying* / *will you have tried* to accomplish next?

**Chris** I (9) *'ll work hard* / *'m going to work hard* to help our team bring in some talented new players. We (10) *'ve been recruiting* / *'ll have recruited* a couple of really great players, and I hope they (11) *'ll be making up* / *'ll have made up* their minds by the end of the year.

**STAR REPORT** Zoe, you already have two children from an earlier marriage. Are you planning any more children with Chris?

**Zoe** Chris is already a great father to my two children, and we (12) *'ll have* / *'ll have had* a child together as soon as the time is right. But for the time being, we (13) *'ll be concentrating* / *'ll have concentrated* on our careers.

**Chris** And I know that I (14) *'ll always have been able to* / *'ll always be able to* count on the support of my lovely wife.

**STAR REPORT** Thank you. Good luck in the future!

**Zoe and Chris** Thank you. ▪

## 6 Correcting mistakes

Put a check (✔) next to the correct sentences. Correct the wrong future forms in the other sentences.

1. ☑ **A** Have you heard? Sue's going to have a baby.

   ☐ **B** Really? ~~I'm going to~~ call her now to
   
   *I'll*
   
   congratulate her.

2. ☐ **A** What do you do this weekend?

   ☐ **B** I don't know yet. Maybe I'll call Paul and see what he's doing.

3. ☐ **A** I'll be honest with you, Matthew. I don't think you're going to pass this exam.

   ☐ **B** Oh, no! What will I be doing?

4. ☐ **A** Is it true that Rachel will get married to that awful boyfriend of hers this weekend?

   ☐ **B** I'm afraid so. And I'm going to the wedding. I have to. I'm her bridesmaid!

5. ☐ **A** Our plane leaves at six o'clock on Saturday morning.

   ☐ **B** Yuck! You have to wake me up. I can never get up in the morning.

6. ☐ **A** It's my birthday on Sunday. I'm going to be 30!

   ☐ **B** Thirty! That's ancient! You are retiring soon.

7. ☐ **A** Mickey and David will be arriving soon, and the house is such a mess.

   ☐ **B** Don't worry. It'll only be taking a few minutes to clean up.

8. ☐ **A** Will you be going skiing as usual this winter?

   ☐ **B** Not this year. It's too expensive. We'll stay at home.

9. ☐ **A** I'll call you as soon as I'll arrive.

   ☐ **B** Please do. We'll be waiting to hear you've arrived safely.

## Conjunctions in time clauses

### 7 Future time clauses

> ❗ 1 Notice that, in clauses after *if, when, as soon as, until, before, after, once,* and *unless,* present tenses are normally used to talk about the future. A future form is not used.
>
> *I'll call you **when I arrive**.* NOT ~~when I'll arrive~~
>
> *I won't marry you **unless you find** a job!*
>
> NOT ~~unless you'll find a job~~
>
> 2 If it is important to show that the first action has not been completed yet, but will be before the second action begins, the Present Perfect is used.
>
> *I'll fax you the report **as soon as I've written** it.*
>
> *They're taking a vacation **after they've saved** enough money.*

Complete the sentences with the verbs in parentheses in the Present Simple, Present Perfect, or a future form.

1. Unless you **eat** (eat) sensibly, you **won't get** (not get) better.

2. We _____ (not move) to Paris until we _____ (find) an apartment there to rent.

3. You _____ (love) Adam when you _____ (meet) him. He's so funny.

4. _____ you _____ (get) your driver's license when you _____ (be) 16?

5. The children _____ (not go) to bed unless they _____ (have) a glass of milk.

6. It _____ (be) at least an hour before I _____ (finish) this report.

7. If you _____ (not do) well on the test, _____ you _____ (have to) do it again?

8. As soon as we _____ (be) able to process the information, we _____ (deal) with your request.

9. The doctor says that I _____ (feel) much better once I _____ (have) the operation.

10. Once you _____ (try) Glowhite toothpaste, you _____ (never use) anything else!

# Vocabulary

## 8 take or put?

**CD 18** Complete the conversation with the correct form of *take* or *put*.

**A** Come in. Make yourself at home. (1) __Put__ some music on.

**B** Thanks, I will. Mmm, something smells nice.

**A** Oh, dinner's (2) _____ forever. Go and sit down. Put your feet up and (3) _____ it easy. It'll be a while before we eat. How's your week been, by the way?

**B** Terrible. My boss is (4) _____ pressure on me to (5) _____ on another project. But I'm already working nonstop, and I'm fed up with (6) _____ work first all the time.

**A** I don't blame you. But the business has really (7) _____ off recently, hasn't it?

**B** Yes, it has, which is great, of course. But I think he'll just have to realize that he needs to (8) _____ on more people now. But he'll never (9) _____ advice from me, of course!

**A** Well, you've been there since the beginning, and I think he just (10) _____ you for granted.

**B** I know. I'm like part of the furniture. I have trouble getting him to (11) _____ any notice of me at all these days.

**A** Oh, don't (12) _____ offense. I'm sure he doesn't mean it like that. He's just too busy, that's all.

**B** Maybe you're right. But he should (13) _____ himself in my shoes once in a while and realize how he makes me feel.

**A** You'll just have to talk to him about it. Anyway, this'll put a smile on your face. Dinner is served!

# Listening

## 9 Thanks for calling

1 **CD 19** Listen to three phone conversations. Mark the sentences true (**T**) or false (**F**).

**Andy and Barry**
1. ☒ **F** Barry is trying to end the conversation.
2. ☐ Andy and Barry probably work together.
3. ☐ Andy has already sent Barry the report.
4. ☐ They are probably talking on a Friday.

**Richard and Tiffany**
5. ☐ Richard is in a good mood.
6. ☐ Richard is calling to cancel his credit card.
7. ☐ Tiffany is trying to sell Richard additional services.
8. ☐ Richard is trying to end the phone call.

**Mario and Amy**
9. ☐ Amy wants to speak to Mario's roommate.
10. ☐ Amy and Mario are good friends.
11. ☐ Amy is trying to end the phone call.
12. ☐ Amy didn't give all of necessary information about the study group.

2 **CD 19** Listen again. Who says these expressions? Write A (Andy), R (Richard), or M (Mario).

1. Thanks so much for calling. __A__
2. I'm in a bit of a hurry today. _____
3. I'll let you go now. _____
4. I've got to run. _____
5. I'm late for a meeting. _____
6. Talk to you soon! _____
7. I really have to go. _____
8. It was good talking to you. _____

# Phrasal verbs

## 10 Types 2 and 3 phrasal verbs

> **!** 1 Both type 2 and type 3 phrasal verbs have an object.
>
> | Type 2 | Type 3 |
> |---|---|
> | *Take off **your coat**.* | *I'll look through **my notes**.* |
> | *I put **the DVD** on.* | *I'll look into **the problem**.* |
>
> 2 In type 2, the particle can be placed before or after the object.
>
> > *Take your coat **off**.*
> > *I put **on** the DVD.*
>
> If the object is a pronoun (*him, it, me*, etc.), the particle comes after it.
>
> > *Take it **off**.* NOT ~~Take off it~~.
> > *I put it **on**.* NOT ~~I put on it~~.
>
> 3 In type 3, the particle is always placed before the object.
>
> > NOT ~~I'll look my notes through.~~
> > ~~I'll look them through.~~
> > ~~I'll look the problem into.~~
> > ~~I'll look it into.~~
>
> 4 Dictionaries usually tell you which type a phrasal verb is.
>
> **put sth on** The particle is shown *after* **sth**. This is type 2.
> **look into sth** The particle is shown *before* **sth**. This is type 3.

Put a pronoun in the correct place in these sentences.

1. Listen to this song. I'll put **it**_____ on _____ for you.
2. I know you have a lot of problems, but I'm sure you'll get _____ through **them**____.
3. I can't remember the directions. I couldn't take _____ all in _____ .
4. There's a problem with my computer. I'll figure _____ out _____ tomorrow.
5. We're having a meeting on the 25th. Put _____ on _____ your calendar.
6. There are clothes all over your bedroom. Please put _____ away _____ .
7. I know this is a problem, but I can't get _____ over _____ .
8. I'm sorry you had a complaint about your room. I'll look _____ into _____ right away.
9. That was a mean thing you said! Take _____ back _____!

# Pronunciation

## 11 Sounds and spelling

1 **CD 20** In each group of words, three words rhyme. <u>Underline</u> the odd one out.

| | | | | | |
|---|---|---|---|---|---|
| 1. | /ʌ/ | done | <u>phone</u> | won | son |
| 2. | /ʊ/ | would | should | good | blood |
| 3. | /u/ | move | love | prove | groove |
| 4. | /oʊ/ | though | through | throw | sew |
| 5. | /eɪ/ | weak | break | ache | shake |
| 6. | /aʊ/ | flower | power | tower | lower |
| 7. | /ər/ | worth | birth | north | earth |
| 8. | /eɪ/ | hate | wait | weight | height |
| 9. | /ɪr/ | fear | near | pear | clear |
| 10. | /ɛr/ | share | bear | fair | hear |
| 11. | /æ/ | bad | plaid | paid | add |
| 12. | /aɪ/ | weigh | high | bye | my |

2 **CD 21** Write the words underlined in Exercise 1 next to their rhymes below. Then listen and check.

1. shown    <u>phone</u>
2. fourth    _____
3. mud    _____
4. might    _____
5. glove    _____
6. air    _____
7. threw    _____
8. here    _____
9. week    _____
10. made    _____
11. thrower    _____
12. play    _____

*"You'd best take off your hat and coat and make yourself comfortable, Milton. It's going to be a long, long marriage."*

# 6 Making it big

**Grammar:** Countable and uncountable nouns • Expressing quantity
**Vocabulary:** *A piece of cake!*
**Pronunciation:** Shifting word stress

## Countable and uncountable nouns

▶▶ **Grammar Reference 6.1 Student Book pp. 142–143**

### 1 Countable or uncountable?

Underline the noun in each group that is usually uncountable.

1. vacation   trip   flight   <u>luggage</u>   suitcase
2. meal   dish   food   menu   dessert
3. check   coin   cash   salary   bonus
4. job   employee   boss   unemployment   profession
5. pop group   musical   music   opera   concert
6. arrest   violence   accident   crime   criminal
7. highway   traffic   traffic jam   lane   rush hour

Underline the noun in each group that is usually countable.

8. luck   happiness   opportunity   fun   help
9. ingredient   cutlery   fruit   meat   food
10. fresh air   sleep   fluid   health   energy

### 2 some or any?

Complete the sentences with *some* or *any*.

1. I did the exercises without **any** help.
2. Would you like _____ more mineral water?
   I don't want _____ more.
3. _____ people don't have _____ problems learning foreign languages.
4. Why don't you ask your father to lend you _____ money? I don't have _____ .
5. My teenage sister never has _____ difficulty learning the words of the latest pop songs. There are hardly _____ she doesn't know by heart.
6. I didn't realize that there was still _____ food left. I've made _____ more.

### 3 much or many?

Rewrite the sentences using the words in parentheses and *much* or *many*. Make any other necessary changes.

1. I'm not sure how much soda to buy. (cans of soda)
   **I'm not sure how many cans of soda to buy.**

2. Are there many jobs to be done in the yard? (work)
   _____

3. I didn't spend many hours on the homework. (time)
   _____

4. Did they do many experiments before they found a cure? (research)
   _____

5. They couldn't give me many details about the delay in our flight. (information)
   _____

6. I didn't have too much difficulty with this exercise. (problems)
   _____

7. I have too many suitcases. I can't carry them all. (luggage)
   _____

8. There are too many cars on the streets of our town. (traffic)
   _____

CHOCOLATE COOKIES · CHOCOLATE CAKE · DONUTS · APPLE PIE

RICE · VEGETABLE CURRY · SPAGHETTI

CHEESE SANDWICHES · CHICKEN SANDWICHES · HAMBURGERS · FRIES · SALAD · FRUIT SALAD · BANANAS · GRAPEFRUIT JUICE · APPLE JUICE · ORANGE JUICE · APPLES

## 4 The cafeteria

**1** Look at the picture of the students' cafeteria. Write ten sentences using each expression in the box once.

| several | a couple of | a few | isn't much |
|---|---|---|---|
| lots of | aren't many | a little | hardly any |
| no | a huge amount of | | |

1. <u>There are several cheese sandwiches.</u>
2. _____
3. _____
4. _____
5. _____
6. _____
7. _____
8. _____
9. _____
10. _____

**2** Look at the picture and answer the students' questions using an expression of quantity without a noun.

1. Is there any chocolate cake?

   Sorry, there's <u>none</u> left.

2. What about rice?

   Well, there's <u>a little</u>.

3. Can I have some spaghetti?

   Yes, of course, there's _____.

4. Do you have lots of chicken sandwiches?

   Well, there are _____.

5. I'd like some orange juice, please.

   Sorry, there isn't _____ left.

6. Can I have some fries with my hamburger?

   Sorry, there aren't _____.

7. Do you have apple pie today?

   Yes, just _____.

8. Are there any chocolate cookies?

   Well, there are _____.

9. Can I have a large serving of fruit salad, please?

   Sorry, there isn't _____ left.

10. Are there any bananas left?

    Yes, I think we have _____.

11. Is this all the apple juice you have?

    Yes, I'm afraid there's only _____.

12. Well, I'll have some grapefruit juice.

    No problem, we have _____.

## 5 *very little, a little, very few, a few, fewer, less*

Rewrite the sentences with *very little, a little, very few, a few, fewer,* or *less*. Change all the <u>underlined</u> words.

1. There was a lot of soda at the party, but <u>hardly any</u> was drunk.  **very little**

2. I'm on a diet, so I'll just have <u>four or five</u> fries.

3. Children <u>don't</u> have <u>as much</u> respect for their teachers <u>as</u> they used to.

4. Lots of people have tried to climb Everest, but <u>not many</u> have succeeded.

5. Dave can speak fluent Portuguese and <u>some</u> Spanish.

6. <u>Not as many</u> people read books these days.

7. <u>Not many</u> people manage to become completely fluent in a language.

8. It's been <u>three or four</u> years since we last saw him.

9. There <u>isn't</u> very <u>much</u> I can do to help you.

10. There are lots of reasons why I don't want the job. Here are <u>some</u> of them.

# Compounds with *some, any, no, every*

## 6 *something, anybody, nowhere, everyone . . .*

> **!**
> 1 *Any, anyone, anybody, anywhere*, and *anything* can mean "it doesn't matter which/who/where/what."
>
> Put the picture **anywhere**, I don't mind.
> You can say **anything** you want. I don't care.
> Borrow **any** book you want.
>
> 2 *Everybody* and *everything* are followed by verbs in the third person singular.
>
> **Everybody** knows who did it.
> **Everything** is ready for the party.

**1** Complete the sentences with a combination of these words.

```
┌──────────┐   ┌──────────────┐
│  some    │   │  one / body  │
│  any     │ + │  thing       │
│  no      │   │  where       │
│  every   │   │              │
└──────────┘   └──────────────┘
```

1. I don't care where we go on vacation as long as it's
   _somewhere_ hot.

2. Does _____ want a cup of tea?

3. I've looked for my contact lens, but I can't find it
   _____.

4. **A** What do you want for dinner, Harry?

   **B** Oh, _____, I don't care!

5. This sale is fantastic. There's 50 percent off
   _____ in the store.

6. It's really boring at Aunt Martha's. There's
   absolutely _____ to do.

7. Our teenage son always complains that
   _____ understands him.

8. There was _____ for me to sit, so I had
   to stand.

9. Jane's getting married to _____ she met
   on her vacation.

10. Sue talks so much! She always has _____ to
    say, but she never says _____ interesting.

11. I love tennis. I'd play with _____.

12. Tommy's so nice. _____ likes him.

**2** Match a line in **A** with a line in **B**.

| A | | B | |
|---|---|---|---|
| 1. **b** He told the police he knew | | a. | anything. |
| 2. ☐ He didn't tell the police | | b. | nothing. |
| 3. ☐ I think they live | | c. | somewhere in Denver. |
| 4. ☐ I don't mind. I'll live | | d. | anywhere in Denver. |
| 5. ☐ Anybody | | e. | called you. Sorry. |
| 6. ☐ Nobody | | f. | can cook. It's easy. |
| 7. ☐ I've searched | | g. | anywhere. |
| 8. ☐ I can't find it | | h. | everywhere. |
| 9. ☐ I thought I'd know | | i. | somebody at the party. |
| 10. ☐ I didn't know | | j. | anyone at the party. |
| 11. ☐ My parents never took me | | k. | everywhere when I was young. |
| 12. ☐ My parents took me | | l. | anywhere when I was a kid. |
| 13. ☐ Jane always got | | m. | everything she wanted. |
| 14. ☐ Jane didn't have | | n. | anything to wear. |
| 15. ☐ I've already had | | o. | something to eat. |
| 16. ☐ I've had | | p. | nothing to eat. |

## Expressing quantity

### 7 Fortune bread

**1** Read and complete the story of Aronda Ochona using the words in the boxes.

# Fortune bread

| ~~much~~ | nobody | a couple | little | few |

Aronda Ochona hasn't had (1) **much** luck in his life—until now, that is. And (2) _____ could have predicted how completely his life would change.

(3) _____ of months ago, 20-year-old Aronda had (4) _____ chance of escaping the grinding poverty in his remote Ugandan village. Now the excited printer's apprentice is busily packing his (5) _____ belongings for his trip to the United States because a multimillionaire is paying for him to study the latest printing techniques.

| any | hardly any | more | all | a bit | part | enough |

Remarkably, Aronda's extraordinary change in fortune is (6) _____ because of a loaf of bread. He explained: "I was hungry, but there wasn't (7) _____ food in the house. I had (8) _____ money—only 100 shillings (6¢), but it was just (9) _____ to buy (10) _____ of bread. The bread is usually wrapped in paper, and that day I saw it was (11) _____ of an American paper, so I took (12) _____ notice.

| none | piece | more than | any | something | no |

On the (13) _____ of paper was an ad for a printing job in Boston. "(14) _____ of my friends have (15) _____ work here. I am training on a printing machine which is (16) _____ 40 years old, and I receive (17) _____ wages. I felt if I was going to make (18) _____ of my life, I had to apply for this job."

| over | a lot | all | several | some | a great deal of |

It took Aronda (19) _____ hours to write the letter and send it. But it turned out that the ad had been placed (20) _____ a year ago. "The company kindly sent me (21) _____ of information about (22) _____ the hi-tech machines they used. I was even more determined to get a chance to work on them."

In the U.S., Aronda's story reached the ears of Conrad Millbank, a tycoon who had made (23) _____ money from publishing. He ordered his lawyers to find the enthusiastic young African. "When I heard that a rich man wanted to pay for my training, I thought it must be a joke. Now I am so happy that I went to buy (24) _____ bread that day."

## Vocabulary

### 8  *A piece of cake!*

1  What combinations can you make using nouns from the two lists?

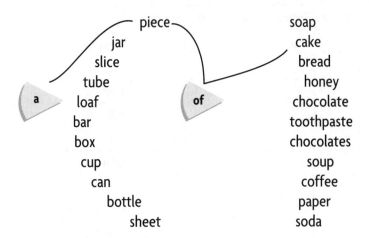

a — piece — of

jar
slice
tube
loaf
bar
box
cup
can
bottle
sheet

soap
cake
bread
honey
chocolate
toothpaste
chocolates
soup
coffee
paper
soda

2  These sentences contain false information about the article on page 38. Correct the mistakes using expressions of quantity.

1. Aronda has quite a lot of money.
   **Aronda has hardly any money.**

2. 100 shillings is a lot of money.
   _____

3. Aronda doesn't have any friends.
   _____

4. Most of his friends have jobs.
   _____

5. It didn't take him much time to write his letter.
   _____

6. There were some printing jobs available at the company.
   _____

7. Nobody heard about his story.
   _____

8. Until now, Aronda has had quite a lot of good fortune in his life.
   _____

2  Replace the underlined words with combinations from Exercise 1.

1. Would you like some cake?
   **Would you like a piece of cake?**

2. All we have for lunch is some soup.
   _____

3. There are two clean pieces of paper on my desk.
   _____

4. Don't forget to buy Mom some chocolates for Mother's Day.
   _____

5. Do you want this chocolate? I don't like this brand.
   _____

6. There's only one bit of bread left.
   _____

7. How much soda was left over from the barbecue?
   _____

8. Hello, reception? This is room 401. There isn't a single bit of soap in the bathroom here.
   _____

9. We brought you some special honey back from the country.
   _____

# Prepositions

## 9 Prepositions and nouns

**1** Which prepositions go with the words on the right in these two charts?

| A | | | | | |
|---|---|---|---|---|---|
| **above** | **below** | **on** | **over** | **under** | |
| ✓ | ✓ | ✓ | | | average |
| | | | | | foot |
| | | | | | arrest |
| | | | | | $500 |
| | | | | | 75% |
| | | | | | freezing |
| | | | | | 18 years old |
| | | | | | new management |
| | | | | | vacation |
| | | | | | pressure |
| | | | | | business |

| B | | | | | |
|---|---|---|---|---|---|
| **at** | **by** | **during** | **in** | **on** | |
| ✓ | ✓ | | | | midnight |
| | | | | | the night |
| | | | | | New Year's Day |
| | | | | | the winter |
| | | | | | Friday afternoon |
| | | | | | the weekend |
| | | | | | time |
| | | | | | the week |
| | | | | | the rush hour |
| | | | | | his forties |

**2** Complete the article with prepositions from Exercise 1.

# Who's that girl?

Gisele Bündchen, the Brazilian model, came to fame (1) __in__ the late 1990s, when she was still (2) _____ 18 years old. (3) _____ the next five years, her face appeared in (4) _____ 100 magazines and fashion campaigns. (5) _____ five feet ten inches tall, she was slightly (6) _____ average height for a fashion model, but she still had the sassiest strut on the catwalk, making about $7,000 an hour (7) _____ average .

In 2004, (8) _____ the height of her career, Gisele actually worked less, turning down (9) _____ 90 percent of the projects offered to her. (10) _____ her year-long absence, she went (11) _____ vacation with her family and acted in her first movie. People wondered if she had been (12) _____ too much pressure, but apparently not. (13) _____ 2007, she had once again become the highest-paid model in the world, having made (14) _____ $33 million that year.

(15) _____ February of 2009, Gisele married American football star Tom Brady in California. (16) _____ the summer, she was already pregnant with their first child, Benjamin. Gisele is aiming for longevity in the short-lived fashion world. So, expect to see her still modeling (17) _____ her fifties!

# Listening

## 10 A business problem

1 **CD 22** Listen to the phone call. Who is calling who? What's the problem?

2 **CD 22** Listen again and mark these sentences true (✔) or false (✗).

1. ☒ James Barker and Ellen Miles don't know each other.
2. ☐ The laptops have not been delivered.
3. ☐ Deliveries usually take more than a week.
4. ☐ James Barker had the order code on hand.
5. ☐ James Barker tells Ellen Miles what went wrong with the order.
6. ☐ James Barker is going to call Ellen Miles in the afternoon.

3 Who says these things? Write **R** (receptionist), **E** (Ellen Miles), or **J** (James Barker).

1. Do you mind holding? _____
2. How's business? _____
3. Can you bear with me? _____
4. Are you ready? _____
5. Can you repeat that last part? _____
6. I'll read that back to you. _____
7. Something's come up. _____
8. I appreciate your time. _____

4 Look at the audio script on p. 83 and find equivalent expressions for these phrases.

1. Who do you want to speak to?
2. I'm connecting you.
3. an order I made
4. no more than a week
5. Do you have the order code with you?
6. That all seems to be correct.
7. I'll call you again.

# Pronunciation

## 11 Shifting word stress

1 **CD 23** Look at the stressed syllable of each word. Write **N** for noun and **V** for verb.

1. ☒V refuse
2. ☐ produce
3. ☐ decrease
4. ☐ progress
5. ☐ insult
6. ☐ permit
7. ☐ record
8. ☐ desert
9. ☐ present
10. ☐ content

2 Read this news item aloud. <u>Underline</u> the stressed syllables in these words.

"Good evening. Here is the news.

Oil <u>imports</u> continued to increase in the last quarter. Demand for fuel is already at record levels, and the president refuses to permit any further increases. Members of the Transportation Workers' Union objected to his criticisms. They insisted they will protest against any possible future sanctions. They presented a report maintaining that present fuel increases are due to a decrease in investment in railway transportation by the government."

3 **CD 24** Listen and check. Practice reading the text again.

4 Read this news item and mark the stress.

"Exports increased in the last quarter due to the present buoyant economy. Government officials are content with the results, calling it the result of decreased regulation for small businesses. They say that the increase in exports will lead to a decrease in unemployment.

In other economic news, tax refunds are on the increase as invalid assessments multiply at the tax office. Tax officials protested against the criticism leveled against them, saying that they were insulted by suggestions that they were not able to produce the correct results. They said they were compiling a report that would present in minute detail the problems they were experiencing since their contract for computer services had been placed with a new company."

5 **CD 25** Listen and check. Practice reading the text again.

# 7 Getting along

**Grammar:** Review of all modals
**Vocabulary:** Money • *get*
**Pronunciation:** Consonant clusters • Sentence stress

## Review of all modals

▶▶ **Grammar Reference 7.1–7.3 Student Book pp. 143–145**

### 1 Meaning check

Put a check (✓) next to the correct explanation for each of these modals.

1. Amy may look for a new job.

   **a.** ☐ Amy has permission to look for a new job.
   **b.** ✓ It's possible that Amy will look for a new job.

2. I couldn't swim until I was 16.

   **a.** ☐ I wasn't allowed to swim until I was 16.
   **b.** ☐ I wasn't able to swim until I was 16.

3. No one can use cell phones in the theater.

   **a.** ☐ No one is able to use cell phones in the theater.
   **b.** ☐ No one is allowed to use cell phones in the theater.

4. You should wear glasses.

   **a.** ☐ My advice is that you wear glasses.
   **b.** ☐ You may have to wear glasses.

5. Will you answer the phone?

   **a.** ☐ Are you at some time in the future going to answer the phone?
   **b.** ☐ I'm asking you to answer the phone.

6. I couldn't get the top off the jar.

   **a.** ☐ I wasn't allowed to get the top off the jar.
   **b.** ☐ I didn't manage to get the top off the jar.

7. You must be tired.

   **a.** ☐ I'm sure you are tired.
   **b.** ☐ You are required to be tired.

8. Andy's very busy, so he may not go to the party.

   **a.** ☐ Andy doesn't have permission to go.
   **b.** ☐ There's a possibility Andy won't go.

## 2 Which modal?

1 Complete the sentences with correct words from the box. Often there is more than one answer.

| will | should | can | ought to | could |
|------|--------|-----|----------|-------|
| must | may | have to | might | |

1. You __should__ get your hair cut. It's too long.
2. _____ I ask you a question?
3. Young children _____ be carried on this escalator.
4. You _____ never get a seat on this train. It's always packed.
5. I _____ be studying Italian next year.
6. I _____ already speak five languages fluently.
7. You'll _____ work much harder if you want to pass.
8. It's Saturday night. There _____ be something good on TV.
9. You _____ leave your jewels in the hotel safe.
10. You _____ be over five feet two inches tall to be a flight attendant.

2 <u>Underline</u> the correct answer.

1. You *can't* / <u>*won't*</u> have any problems with Scott. He's such a good baby.
2. You *don't have to* / *can't* use cream in this sauce, but it makes it much tastier.
3. I *couldn't* / *wouldn't* watch my favorite TV show because Mia called me for a long chat.
4. Ben's so stubborn. He just *can't* / *won't* do what he's told.
5. I'm afraid I *can't* / *may not* come to your wedding. I'll be in Australia.
6. I *was able to* / *could* get 20 percent off the price in the sale.
7. You *don't have to* / *can't* say a word about this to your mother. It's a surprise.

## 3 Affirmative to negative

Rewrite the sentences to make them negative.

1. You must stop here.  <u>You can't stop here.</u>

2. We have to learn the whole poem.  _____

3. They had to take off their shoes.  _____

4. He must be speaking French.  _____

5. We had to wear a uniform at school.  _____

6. You'll have to help me do this exercise.  _____

# Verbs related to modals

## 4 Online helpline

1 Read the web page and replace the words in *italics* with a modal verb, or an expression with a modal verb.

# *Online helpline*

**Your questions answered confidentially**

 *E-mail* Ken Lee

---

**From:** Johana, Los Angeles

**Subject: He's gadget obsessed**

I'm really worried about my friend. He always (1) *feels it's necessary to have* the latest high-tech gear. And he's getting worse. Now, if someone doesn't have the newest cell phone, he (2) *refuses* to call or text them. He's losing touch with reality. He (3) *promised to* have lunch with me the other day, but then he (4) *wasn't able to* because (5) *it was necessary for him* to go to an electronics expo. As a good friend, (6) *is it a good idea if* I talk to him about it?

As a good friend, (7) *it is essential that you* talk to him about it. This gadget thing is certainly concealing a strong inferiority complex, and (8) *maybe he'll* find it hard to discuss it. But if you (9) *manage to* persuade him that he can enjoy life without gadgets, then you (10) *are certain to* do him a huge service.

---

**From:** Mike, Philadelphia

**Subject: I need to exercise!**

I (11) *am able to* get a discount on health insurance at work if I exercise regularly, but I find it difficult. I (12) *'m obliged to* work until late at night, and when I get home I'm tired, and I just (13) *am not able to* go to the gym. (14) *It's also necessary that I* get more exercise for my health because I'm overweight, and I know I (15) *'m sure to have* health problems in the future if I don't get in shape. What do you suggest?

Choose a day and just start exercising. (16) *It's possible that you'll* find it difficult at first, but persevere. Start with something easy, like walking. (17) *It's very necessary that you don't* get discouraged. When I started exercising a few years ago, I (18) *wasn't able to* run a marathon right away, but I felt better every day. (19) *If I were you, I'd* bring a gym bag to work. That way, you (20) *are able to* go straight from the office to the gym. Good luck!

**2** Rewrite the sentences using the words in parentheses.

1. It's Anna's birthday tomorrow, so I should buy her a card.
   ('d better) <u>It's Anna's birthday tomorrow, so I'd better buy her a card.</u>

2. Guests shouldn't leave valuables in their room.  (advised not)
   _____

3. You can only use cell phones in designated areas.  (permitted)
   The use of cell phones _____

4. He'll pass the test. He's so smart.  (sure)
   _____

5. You can't use dictionaries on this test.  (allowed)
   The use of dictionaries _____

6. People under 16 shouldn't drive.  (supposed)
   _____

7. Travelers to this country need a visa.  (required)
   _____

8. I expect you'll find it difficult to learn Chinese.  (likely)
   _____

9. I can't come out. I said I'd help Janet.  (promised)
   _____

10. I wasn't allowed to go out until I was 18.  (let)
    My parents _____

# Modal verbs of probability

## 5  Present probability

**1** Respond to the statements or questions using the words in parentheses. Put the verbs in their correct form.

1. Harry is packing his suitcase.  (must, go on vacation)

   <u>He must be going on vacation.</u>

2. Dina looks really unhappy.  (must, miss, boyfriend)
   _____

3. Who's at the front door?  (must, be, Tom)
   _____

4. Where's Laurie? It's nearly lunchtime!  (can't, still, sleep)
   _____

5. Why are all the lights on in their house?  (could, have, party)
   _____

6. Bob has been working all night.  (must, deadline, to meet)
   _____

7. It's been snowing all night.  (might, difficult, drive, work)
   _____

8. Jason can't find his little sister.  (may, hide, in the yard)
   _____

**2** Complete the conversations with the correct form of the verbs in parentheses.

1. **A** You really (1) <u>should go</u> (should / go) to bed now, or you (2) <u>might feel</u> (might / feel) tired tomorrow.

   **B** I'll go in a minute. I (3) _____ (must / finish) this chapter first.

   **A** You (4) _____ (will / pass) the test easily. Get some rest now.

2. **A** It's 11:05. Louis and Nancy's plane (5) _____ (should / touch down) at Kennedy Airport right now.

   **B** Your watch (6) _____ (must / be) slow. It's nearly 11:30.

   **A** It (7) _____ (can not / be)! I just had it repaired.

3. **A** Bring very warm clothes. It (8) _____ (could / snow) when we arrive.

   **B** Oh, yes. I've heard it (9) _____ (can / snow) in the mountains even during the summer.

4. **A** What are all those people doing with those lights and cameras?

   **B** They (10) _____ (must / make) a movie.

   **A** Who's the lead actor?

   **B** Not sure. It (11) _____ (might / be) him over there. And do you think that she's the lead actress?

   **A** She (12) _____ (could / be). She's certainly beautiful enough!

# Vocabulary

## 6 Money

**1** Match a line in **A** with a line in **B**.

| A | B |
|---|---|
| 1. **e** My checking account | a. will take years to pay off. |
| 2. ☐ I opened | b. a savings account. |
| 3. ☐ His debts | c. good right now. |
| 4. ☐ I changed | d. debts of $2,000. |
| 5. ☐ Inflation | e. is overdrawn. |
| 6. ☐ He accumulated | f. to the household bills. |
| 7. ☐ My credit card | g. went up by 2%. |
| 8. ☐ She contributes | h. in interest. |
| 9. ☐ The exchange rate is | i. some traveler's checks. |
| 10. ☐ I made $2,000 | j. expires at the end of July. |

**2** Read the story and <u>underline</u> the most suitable words.

**Ben** stood at the (1) *check-in / checkout* at the supermarket as the cashier (2) *summed / added* up his (3) *bill / fees*. It came to $72.67, and she asked him how he would like to (4) *pay / cost*.

Ben didn't have much money in his bank account because he hadn't been paid yet, so if he paid (5) *by check / in cash*, he would be (6) *overdrawn / overdue*. Then he realized he had left his (7) *credit card / money* at home. And he couldn't afford to pay (8) *cash / money* because he only had $60.

The cashier told him that if he exchanged many of the items he had bought for the supermarket's own brand, he would (9) *reduce / accumulate* his bill by as much as 25 percent. So Ben set off around the store again.

His new bill (10) *added / came to* only $56.50—a (11) *savings / discount* of $16.17. Ben got $3.50 (12) *change / coins* from his $60 and his new (13) *receipt / recipe*.

## 7 *get*

Complete the conversation with the expressions in the box. Put the verb in the correct form.

| | | |
|---|---|---|
| get all these calls | get around | get my hair |
| get someone to help | get through | ~~get up~~ |
| get to the office | get too excited | |

**A** Hi, Barbara. What's the matter?

**B** Oh, so many things! It has been a horrible day. I (1) **got up** late and didn't have time to (2) _____ cut as I had planned. Then the traffic was terrible, and it took me two hours to (3) _____. And now I've been (4) _____ from customers complaining about the new software. I can't even (5) _____ to reading my e-mails!

**A** Calm down. Just (6) _____ you with the calls.

**B** I tried, but so many people seem to be away today. And those who are in have been as busy as I am.

**A** OK, let me just (7) _____ some documents I need to read, and I'll help you.

**B** Thank you so much, Alison. I really appreciate it.

**A** But don't (8) _____. I can only help you for an hour.

# Phrasal verbs

## 8 Type 4 phrasal verbs

 **1** Type 4 phrasal verbs have a verb + adverb + preposition. The preposition is followed by an object.

*Do you **get along with** your neighbors?*
*We've **run out of** sugar.*

**2** The word order cannot change.

*Do you **get along with** them?*
NOT ~~Do you get along them with?~~
*We've **run out of** it.*
NOT ~~We've run out it of.~~

**3** Dictionaries usually show type 4 phrasal verbs by giving both the adverb and the preposition.

**get away with sth**

**4** Sometimes a phrasal verb can be type 4 or type 1. In these cases, dictionaries usually show this.

**break up (with sb)**

*They **broke up** after a five-year marriage.*
*She's sad because she's just **broken up with** her boyfriend.*

Complete the sentences with the combinations in the box.

| away with | off with (× 2) | up for | up with | out of |
|-----------|----------------|--------|---------|--------|
| along with | out with | ~~up to~~ | down on | on with |

1. Joey! You have a very guilty look on your face! What bad things have you been **up to** this time?

2. The thief broke into the house and made _____ a lot of jewelry.

3. We must try to cut _____ the amount of money we spend every month. We spend more than we make.

4. Don't let me disturb you. Go _____ your work.

5. I'm sorry we couldn't get tickets for the play. I'll take you to a restaurant to make _____ it. Does that cheer you up?

6. There is a move in Britain to do _____ the monarchy completely so that Britain would become a republic.

7. Sam's so stingy with money. He's always trying to get _____ paying his share of the bills for the apartment.

8. I went _____ Angela for two years, and then she suddenly went _____ someone else without saying anything!

9. I can't stand Larry. I can't put _____ his rudeness a minute longer. I'm leaving him.

10. Judith's a very difficult person to get _____ . She's always having arguments with people. I'm leaving her.

BREAKING UP

Judith: *I can't stand Larry. I'm leaving him.*

Larry: *Judith's a very difficult person. I'm leaving her.*

# Listening

## 9 Not getting along

**1** **CD 26** Listen to the conversation and choose the best answer.

| | | |
|---|---|---|
| 1. Sophie's upset about … | a. ☐ b. ☐ c. ☐ | her friend. the evening. her boyfriend. |
| 2. Ted's … | a. ☐ b. ☐ c. ☐ | ignored Sophie. been mean to Sophie. laughed at Sophie. |
| 3. Ted's … | a. ☐ b. ☐ c. ☐ | out of work. looking for a new job. having problems at work. |
| 4. Anya wants Sophie to … | a. ☐ b. ☐ c. ☐ | leave Ted. be nice to Ted. tell Ted to stop it. |
| 5. Sophie … | a. ☐ b. ☐ c. ☐ | agrees to this. doesn't want to. wants things to get magically better. |

**2** **CD 26** Listen again and complete these understatements.

1. I'm just _____ , that's all.
2. He made _____ remarks this evening.
3. He's been having _____ recently.
4. It's getting me _____ .
5. Our relationship _____ lately.

# Pronunciation

## 10 Consonant clusters

English has many words with groups (or clusters) of consonants:

happened
couldn't
puzzles

**CD 27** Listen to these words and write them. They all have consonant clusters.

1. _____    6. _____
2. _____    7. _____
3. _____    8. _____
4. _____    9. _____
5. _____    10. _____

## 11 Sentence stress

**CD 28** Alan and Kevin are talking about Frank. Read the conversation aloud and mark the stress in Kevin's responses.

1. **Alan** Don't you think Frank's put on a lot of weight recently?

   **Kevin** You're kidding. If anything, he's lost weight.

2. **Alan** I think Frank makes more than me.

   **Kevin** Well, I know he makes a lot more than me.

3. **Alan** He's thinking of buying a second-hand Mercedes.

   **Kevin** What do you mean? He's already bought a brand new one.

4. **Alan** He's just bought two pairs of designer jeans.

   **Kevin** Didn't you know that all Frank's clothes are designer labels?

5. **Alan** Does Frank have many stocks and bonds?

   **Kevin** He has lots of them.

6. **Alan** Isn't Frank in New York on business?

   **Kevin** No, in fact, he's in California on vacation.

7. **Alan** His latest girlfriend has long blond hair.

   **Kevin** Really? The girl I saw him with had short brown hair.

# 8 People and places

**Grammar:** Defining and nondefining relative clauses
**Vocabulary:** People, places, and things
**Pronunciation:** Silent consonants

## Defining and nondefining relative clauses

▶▶ **Grammar Reference 8.1 Student Book pp. 145–146**

### 1 General knowledge quiz
Put a check (✓) next to the correct answer.

> ## Test Your Knowledge of People and Places
>
> 1. **Death Valley,**
>    a. ☐ *which is in Arizona,*
>    b. ☐ *which is in California,*
>    c. ☐ *which is in Texas,*
>    **is the hottest place in North America.**
>
> 2. **The Galactic Suite Space Resort,**
>    a. ☐ *which will cost $2.3 million a night,*
>    b. ☐ *which will cost $4.4 million for three nights,*
>    c. ☐ *which will cost $10 million a week,*
>    **will be the most expensive hotel ever created.**
>
> 3. **American Philip Parker,**
>    a. ☐ *who has created over 2,000 books,*
>    b. ☐ *who has created over 20,000 books,*
>    c. ☐ *who has created over 200,000 books,*
>    **is the world's most prolific author—he uses a computer program that automatically "writes" his books.**
>
> 4. **Kilimanjaro,**
>    a. ☐ *which is the highest summit in Africa and Asia,*
>    b. ☐ *which is the highest summit in Africa,*
>    c. ☐ *which is the highest summit in the world,*
>    **is in Tanzania.**
>
> 5. **The city that has the most people per sq. km. is**
>    a. ☐ *Beijing, China.*
>    b. ☐ *Mumbai, India.*
>    c. ☐ *Mexico City, Mexico.*
>
> 6. **The highest waterfall in the world, which is called**
>    a. ☐ *Angel Falls,*
>    b. ☐ *Niagara Falls,*
>    c. ☐ *Victoria Falls,*
>    **is in Venezuela.**
>
> 7. **Bambuti pygmies, who only live in the African rain forest,**
>    a. ☐ *are the tallest people in the world.*
>    b. ☐ *are the smallest people in the world.*
>    c. ☐ *are the thinnest people in the world.*
>
> 8. **The driest place on earth is the Atacama Desert,**
>    a. ☐ *which is in Egypt.*
>    b. ☐ *which is in Europe.*
>    c. ☐ *which is in Chile.*

## 2 Defining or nondefining?

**1** Decide if these sentences are best completed with a defining relative clause (D) or a nondefining relative clause (ND). Write **D** or **ND** in the boxes.

1. [ D ] I'd love to meet someone <u>who could teach me</u> <u>how to cook</u>.

2. [  ] We're looking for a house _____ _____.

3. [  ] We went to see *Romeo and Juliet* _____ _____.

4. [  ] Do you know a store _____ _____?

5. [  ] Marilyn Monroe _____ _____ was one of the most famous actresses of her time.

6. [  ] I find people _____ difficult to get along with.

7. [  ] My computer _____ is already out of date.

8. [  ] I met a girl _____.

9. [  ] Professor James Williams _____ _____ will give a talk next week.

10. [  ] I bought a roast beef sandwich _____ _____.

**2** Complete the sentences in Exercise 1 with this information. Add a relative pronoun and commas where necessary. Leave out the relative pronoun if possible.

> You went to school with her.
>
> I ate it immediately.
>
> It has four bedrooms.
>
> I bought it just last year.
>
> They lose their temper.
>
> It sells second-hand furniture.
>
> Her real name was Norma Jean Baker.
>
> This person could teach me how to cook.
>
> We really enjoyed it.
>
> Many people consider him to be the world's biggest expert on volcanoes.

## 3 Punctuation and omitting the pronoun

Add commas to these sentences if they have a nondefining relative clause. Cross out the pronoun in the defining relative clauses if possible.

1. Sheila, who I first got to know at college, was one of six children.

2. The man ~~who~~ you were talking to is a famous artist.

3. This is the story that amazed the world. (no change)

4. The thing that I most regret is not going to college.

5. My two daughters who are 16 and 13 are both interested in dancing.

6. The town where I was born has changed dramatically.

7. I didn't like the clothes that were on sale.

8. Salt that comes from the sea is considered to be the best for cooking.

9. Salt whose qualities have been known since prehistoric times is used to season and preserve food.

10. The CD that I bought yesterday doesn't work.

11. The part of Europe where I'd most like to live is Portugal.

12. The Algarve where my mother's family comes from is famous for its beautiful beaches and dramatic coastline.

## 4  All relative pronouns

**1**  Match a line in **A** with a line in **B**.

| A | B |
|---|---|
| 1. [*e*] Have I told you recently | a. when you expect to arrive. |
| 2. ☐ I have to do | b. where my brother lives. |
| 3. ☐ We were stuck in traffic for seven hours, | c. which came as a bit of a surprise. |
| 4. ☐ We're emigrating to Australia, | d. whose hair came down to her waist. |
| 5. ☐ I met a girl | e. how much I love you? |
| 6. ☐ I passed all the tests, | f. whatever you want. |
| 7. ☐ Let me know | g. which was a nightmare. |
| 8. ☐ Being generous, I'll buy you | h. what I believe to be right. |

**2**  Complete the sentences with *who, which, that, where, whose,* or *whatever.* If the pronoun can be omitted, add nothing. Sometimes more than one pronoun is possible.

1. The lady **who** is sitting in the wheelchair is my grandmother.
2. I know an Italian restaurant _____ serves excellent pasta.
3. I know an Italian restaurant _____ you can always get a table.
4. Uncle Arthur makes a fortune, _____ is why I've asked him to lend me $10,000.
5. Sandra is a child _____ people immediately like.
6. My daughter, _____ ambition is to emigrate to Australia, has finally received her visa.
7. I gave him a glass of water, _____ he drank thirstily.
8. The flight _____ we wanted to get was fully booked.
9. My aunt's house is the place _____ I feel most at home.
10. This is the smallest car _____ has ever been made.
11. That's the man _____ wife left him because he kept his pet snake in their bedroom.
12. I love the things _____ you say to me.
13. I go shopping at the new mall, _____ there's always free parking.
14. She told me she'd been married before, _____ I didn't realize.
15. _____ you do, don't touch that button. The machine will explode.

## 5  Prepositions in relative clauses

Combine the sentences, keeping the preposition after the verb in the relative clause.

1. I want you to meet the people. I work with them.

   **I want you to meet the people I work with.**

2. She's a friend. I can always rely on her.

   _____

   _____

3. That's the man. The police were looking for him.

   _____

   _____

4. She recommended a book by Robert Palmer. I'd never heard of him.

   _____

   _____

5. You paid $400 for a suit. It has been reduced to $200.

   The suit _____

   _____

6. This is the book. I was telling you about it.

   _____

   _____

7. The president gave a good speech. I agree with his views.

   _____

   _____

8. He spoke about the environment. I care deeply about this.

   _____

   _____

9. What's that music? You're listening to it.

   _____

   _____

10. His mother died last week. He took care of her for many years.

   _____

   _____

# Participles

▶▶ **Grammar Reference 8.2 Student Book p. 146**

## 6 Participles as adjectives

Complete the adjectives with -*ed* or -*ing*.

1. a shock**ing** story
2. a reserv**ed** seat
3. scream____ children
4. a satisfi____ customer
5. a disgust____ meal
6. a confus____ explanation
7. a concern____ parent
8. a conceit____ person
9. a frighten____ movie
10. an exhaust____ walk
11. disappoint____ grades
12. a tir____ trip
13. an unexpect____ surprise
14. disturb____ news
15. a thrill____ story
16. a relax____ vacation
17. a disappoint____ customer
18. well-behav____ children
19. a promis____ start
20. a cake load____ with calories

## 7 Participle clauses

1 Rewrite the sentences with a present or past participle clause instead of a relative clause.

1. Can you see the woman who's dressed in red over there?

   <u>Can you see the woman dressed in red over there?</u>

2. People who live in apartment buildings often complain of loneliness.

   _____

3. Letters that are mailed before 5 P.M. should arrive the next day.

   _____

4. The train that is leaving from platform 7 is going to Albany.

   _____

5. Firefighters have rescued passengers who were trapped in the accident.

   _____

6. They live in a charming house that overlooks the Hudson River.

   _____

7. It took workmen days to clean up the trash that was left by the crowds.

   _____

2 Complete each sentence with a verb from the box in either its present or past participle form.

| feel | borrow | explain | say | ~~ruin~~ | study | finish | take | know | steal |
|------|--------|---------|-----|----------|-------|--------|------|------|-------|

1. Jo was in a bad mood for the whole week, completely **ruining** our vacation.
2. After _____ her tests, Meg went out to celebrate.
3. Jewelry _____ in the robbery has never been recovered.
4. I got a letter from the lawyer _____ that I owe him $5,000.
5. _____ hungry, I decided to make myself a sandwich.
6. Books _____ from the library must be returned in two weeks.
7. Not _____ what to do, she burst out crying.
8. I had a long talk with Ron, _____ why it was important for him to work hard.
9. _____ everything into consideration, I've decided to give you a second chance.
10. With both children _____ for tests, the house was really quiet.

# Review of relatives and participles

## 8 The thrill seeker

**CD 29** Read and complete the article with the clauses in the box.

### Relative clause

a. where temperatures drop to −71°C

b. who battles with

c. who sees that as a challenge

d. that nature ever invented

e. in which there is a lake of boiling lava

f. where everyone else is

g. no one has done before

h. you've never heard of before

i. which unexpectedly develops

### Past participle

j. otherwise known as

k. Trapped for five days

### Present participle

l. before heading for the high winds

m. starting this Monday on the Discovery Channel

n. getting right inside the 150mph winds

# The thrill seeker

## He laughs in the face of common sense. He is …

### DANGERMAN

"It helps to be fearless."

So says Dangerman, (1) __j__ extreme adventure cameraman, Geoff Mackley, (2) ____ some of the most inhospitable weather conditions and desolate places (3) ____ . What drives the New Zealander to do it?

"There aren't many places left where no one has ever been, or things (4) ____ , and I'm one of those people (5) ____ !" he says.

See for yourself in his series of daredevil adventures, (6) ____ .

---

EPISODE 1 **The Perfect Storm**

■ Dangerman chases after major typhoons, first in Asia, (7) ____ of North Carolina, and finally (8) ____ of Hurricane Isabel.

---

EPISODE 2 **The Deep Freeze**

■ In the coldest town on earth, in Northern Siberia, (9) ____ , Dangerman and extreme survival expert Mark Whetu become the first people to camp outside!

---

EPISODE 3 **The Crater's Edge**

■ Dangerman climbs down into a volcano, (10) ____ , and gets caught in a tropical storm (11) ____ into a cyclone. (12) ____ with no food or water, he survives torrential rain, violent winds, and clouds of toxic gas.

■ Dangerman says: "Who wants to be (13) ____ ? It's the thrill of finding a place (14) ____ . More people have landed on the moon than have been to these places."

# Vocabulary

## 9 People, places, and things

**1** Complete the chart with these descriptive adjectives. Put six in each group.

| | | | | |
|---|---|---|---|---|
| ~~unspoiled~~ | stubborn | breathtaking | thrilled | spoiled |
| aggressive | picturesque | automatic | handmade | deserted |
| exhausted | accurate | waterproof | desolate | long-lasting |
| priceless | easygoing | overcrowded | | |

| People | Places | Things |
|---|---|---|
| | unspoiled | |
| | | |
| | | |
| | | |
| | | |
| | | |

**2** Complete each sentence with an adjective from Exercise 1.

1. The view from the top of the mountain was absolutely **breathtaking** —fantastic scenery as far as the eye could see.

2. These flowers are pretty _____ if you keep the vase full of water and in the shade.

3. The new car we bought is fully _____ . I don't want to change gears when I'm driving anymore.

4. You're good to travel with. You're very _____ and don't worry about anything.

5. The countryside we camped in was completely _____ —not a person, a store, or a campground for miles.

6. The Cotswolds is an area in England which is very _____ . It has lots of pretty, old-fashioned villages and beautiful green countryside.

7. Their child is really _____ . He won't do a thing they tell him. I think it's because he's _____ . They give him everything he asks for.

8. That bag you're looking at is _____ . Look at the quality of the work.

9. The beach was seriously _____ . There was no room to put our towels down, so we rented a boat and sailed along the coast until we found a tiny one which was completely _____ . We were the only ones on it!

# Listening

## 10 Extreme weather

**1** **CD 30** Listen to two people, Alex and Sam, talk about their experiences with extreme weather. Who are these statements true for? Write **A** (Alex), **S** (Sam), or **B** (both).

1. The weather was rainy. **B**_____

2. The story takes place in Chicago. _____

3. The wind was strong. _____

4. The speaker's clothes were ruined. _____

5. The speaker felt embarrassed. _____

6. The speaker was laughing at the time. _____

**2** **CD 30** Listen again. Complete the comments with *which*.

1. I went camping with my wife, Judy, **which was a bad idea because I just knew she'd hate it** .

2. … the weather report said there was a good chance of rain, _____ .

3. Judy started crying, saying she was scared, _____ .

4. I was doing this summer internship, _____

5. I had to save money by riding my bike to work, _____

6. My clothes really got soaking wet, _____

# Prepositions

## 11 Adjective + preposition

Complete these sentences with the correct preposition.

1. Are you afraid _of_ the dark?
2. She was angry _____ me _____ not telling her the news.
3. Milan is famous _____ its design.
4. Phil is jealous _____ me because I'm smarter than him.
5. I'm very proud _____ my two daughters.
6. I'm disappointed _____ you. I thought I could trust you.
7. You're very different _____ your brother.
   I thought you'd be similar _____ each other.
8. Are you excited _____ going to Rome?
9. She was not used _____ such a humid summer.
10. Visitors to hot countries need to be aware _____ the risk of malaria.
11. You should be ashamed _____ what you did.
12. I am most grateful _____ all your help.
13. Who is responsible _____ this mess?
14. What's wrong _____ you? You don't look well.
15. My son is crazy _____ a rock group called The Foo Fighters.

# Pronunciation

## 12 Silent consonants

1 English words often have silent consonants:

~~k~~now      ~~w~~riter      wal~~k~~      clim~~b~~

**CD 31** Complete the chart with the words from the box. Cross out the silent consonants.

| ~~industry~~ | executive | ~~honest~~ | inhabitant |
|---|---|---|---|
| receipt | distinctly | rebuilt | fasten |
| eccentric | insect | lamp | sumptuous |
| exhausted | whistle | straight | anonymous |
| citizen | fascinating | delighted | documentary |
| landscape | tomb | castle | debt |

| A | B |
|---|---|
| **all consonants pronounced** | **some consonants not pronounced** |
| industry | ~~h~~onest |

2 **CD 32** Complete the words with the silent consonants.

1. s _c_ ientific
2. _____sychologist
3. han_____some
4. recei_____t
5. Chris_____mas
6. ni_____htmare
7. clim_____
8. gran_____father
9. We_____nesday
10. thum_____

# 9 Changing times

**Grammar:** Present and past habit •
*used to, be used to,* and *get used to*
**Vocabulary:** Homonyms • Homophones
**Pronunciation:** Weak and strong forms

## Present and past habit

▶▶ **Grammar Reference 9.1 Student Book p. 152**

### 1 Present habit

**1** Match a sentence in **A** with a sentence in **B**.

| A | B |
|---|---|
| 1. [d] She's really generous. | a. He's always applying for new jobs. |
| 2. ☐ He's so disorganized. | b. She never thinks before she speaks. |
| 3. ☐ She's very fashionable. | c. He won't ever change his mind. |
| 4. ☐ He's so dishonest. | d. She's always buying me presents. |
| 5. ☐ She's so sensitive. | e. He's always telling lies. |
| 6. ☐ He's really stubborn. | f. She'll only wear designer clothes. |
| 7. ☐ She's so rude. | g. He never finishes anything he starts. |
| 8. ☐ They're so spoiled. | h. She'll start crying at the slightest thing. |
| 9. ☐ She's very energetic. | i. They get everything they ask for. |
| 10. ☐ He's very ambitious. | j. She jogs to work every day. |

**2** Write more sentences like those in column **B** above. Use either the Present Simple, *always* + Present Continuous, or *will*.

1. She's very fussy about her food. <u>**She never eats anything you make for her.**</u>

2. He's really arrogant. _____

3. She adores ice cream. _____

4. He hates all sports. _____

5. He's a real computer geek. _____

6. She's a TV addict! _____

7. He's really easygoing. _____

8. They are so clumsy. _____

9. He's very kind. _____

### 2 Past habit

**1** Complete the sentences with the correct form of *used to*: affirmative, negative, or question.

1. There <u>used to</u> be a beautiful old building where the parking lot is now.

2. _____ (you) have a part-time job when you were in school?

3. She _____ be so moody. It's only since she lost her job.

4. _____ (you) play volleyball when you were younger?

5. My grandfather never _____ get so out of breath when he climbed the stairs.

6. Julie _____ be as slim as she is now. She's been dieting.

7. Where _____ (you) go out to eat when you lived in Madrid?

8. _____ (you) run five miles a day? Why did you quit?

**2** Which of the verb forms can complete the sentences below and keep them in the past? Put a check (✔) next to all the possible answers.

1. I _____ long blond hair when I was first married.
   a. ✔ had   b. ✔ used to have   c. ☐ would have

2. We _____ Jessica every time we went to Atlanta.
   a. ☐ visited   b. ☐ used to visit   c. ☐ would visit

3. Pam _____ out with Dan for six months, but then she broke up with him.
   a. ☐ went   b. ☐ used to go   c. ☐ would go

4. We _____ coffee and croissants every morning for breakfast.
   a. ☐ had   b. ☐ used to have   c. ☐ would have

5. We _____ to each other every day when we were apart.
   a. ☐ wrote   b. ☐ used to write   c. ☐ would write

6. He _____ to me for 25 years and then stopped.
   a. ☐ wrote   b. ☐ used to write   c. ☐ would write

7. In the old days people _____ you if you were in trouble.
   a. ☐ helped   b. ☐ used to help   c. ☐ would help

8. I _____ living so close to the sea.
   a. ☐ loved   b. ☐ used to love   c. ☐ would love

9. Dave _____ Molly three times if she wanted to go out with him.
   a. ☐ asked   b. ☐ used to ask   c. ☐ would ask

10. I _____ questions in class. I was too shy.
   a. ☐ never asked   b. ☐ never used to ask   c. ☐ would never ask

**3** Annoying behavior

**1** Put a check (✔) next to the sentences where the speaker is annoyed by someone's behavior. The words in italics are emphasized in speaking.

1. ☐ He watches all the sports programs on TV.
2. ☐ He's *always* watching sports programs on TV.
3. ☐ She'd give us extra lessons after school.
4. ☐ She *would* give us extra lessons after school.
5. ☐ She was *always* giving us extra lessons.
6. ☐ She used to give us extra lessons.
7. ☐ The cat always sleeps on my bed.
8. ☐ The cat *will* sleep on my bed.
9. ☐ The cat's *always* sleeping on my bed.

**2** Rewrite the sentences below so that they express a criticism.

## My family's bad habits

1. My dad fixes his motorcycle in the living room.
   My dad is always fixing his motorcycle in the living room.

2. My brother leaves the top off the toothpaste.
   _____
   _____

3. My sister often borrows my clothes without asking.
   _____
   _____

4. Uncle Tom combs his hair in the kitchen.
   _____
   _____

5. My grandpa used to eat toast in bed.
   _____
   _____

6. My grandma didn't use to turn on her hearing aid.
   _____
   _____

## 4 *used to*, *be used to*, and *get used to*

> **1** Compare these sentences.
>
> *Don't worry. You'll **get used to** working such long hours.*
> *I **am used to** working long hours, I've done it for years.*
>
> *He eventually **got used to** the tropical climate, but it took a long time.*
> *I was born in India, so I'**m used to** a hot climate.*
>
> *Get used to* means "become used to" and describes a change of state. *Be used to* describes a state.
>
> **2** *Get* can be used with other past participles and adjectives to describe changes of state.
>
> *The ocean's **getting rough**. Let's go back!*
> *We **got lost** on the mountain.*
> *We **got married** last week.*
>
> **3** *Get* can sometimes be used with an infinitive to talk about a gradual change.
>
> *As I **got to know** Paris, I started to like it more and more.*
> *I'm sure the kids will soon **get to like** each other.*

**1** Complete the sentences with *used to*, *be used to*, or *get used to* in the correct form, affirmative or negative.

1. If you **aren't used to** Indian food, this dish might be too spicy for you.

2. I'll never _____ your hair that short. You'll have to grow it again.

3. **A** How do you drive in all this traffic?
   **B** I _____ it now, so it's OK. But it took me a while to _____ all the cars, lanes, and bad tempers, believe me!

4. Matt didn't like his new school at first, but he eventually _____ it and made new friends.

5. I _____ jog every morning, but I don't any more. I'm so out of shape now.

6. When I was a boy, I _____ like going to piano lessons, so I stopped. Now that I'm in my forties, I've started learning again!

7. Sally won't find it easy to go on a diet. She _____ having three spoonfuls of sugar in her coffee!

8. **A** I hate my new job!
   **B** Give it a chance. You may _____ it after you've been there a little longer.

9. _____ you _____ watch old Elvis Presley movies on TV when you were young?

10. **A** _____ you _____ your new teacher yet? I know you didn't like her much at first.
    **B** Well, I have a little. She's OK, I suppose.

**2** Complete the sentences with *get* or *be* in the correct form and a word or expression from the box.

| better | ready (× 2) | dressed | dark | tired | to like |
|--------|-------------|---------|------|-------|---------|
| to know | a pilot | lost | ~~upset~~ | divorced | |

1. I often **get upset** when I watch the news. Such awful things are happening in the world.

2. **A** How are you feeling?
   **B** I _____ slowly, but I still feel weak.

3. My little nephew is determined _____ when he grows up.

4. **A** Come on, Helen! The play starts in half an hour.
   **B** I _____ in two minutes. I _____ just _____ and putting my shoes on.
   **A** I don't know why it takes you so long. I _____ since 6:00.

5. **A** Do we turn right or left at the next intersection?
   **B** I have no idea! I think we _____ .

6. **A** Did you hear that Liz and Chris _____ ?
   **B** No! I always thought they were the perfect couple.

7. I didn't use to like Ray at all, but the more I _____ him, the more I _____ him. Now he's my best friend!

8. Can we stop walking for a minute? I need to rest. I _____ .

9. In the summer it is still light at 9:00 in the evening, but in the winter it _____ at 5:00.

## 5 Do you remember?

**1** Read Sally's e-mail to her old high school friend,
Alison. Which of the verbs in italics …

  a. … can change to *used to*?

  b. … must stay in the Past Simple?

Put the correct letter *a* or *b* next to the verbs.

From:    Sally Davis <sallydavis@yoohoo.com>
Date:    Tues, Sep 18 10:11 AM
To:    AliWright72@yoohoo.com
Subject:  RE: Springfield East

Hi, Alison!

Wow, it's so great to hear from you! Of course I remember you!
You (1) __b__ *had* on that bright yellow sweater the first day we
met, all those years ago, and I remember I (2) __ *was* so jealous.
No one else in school (3) __ *dressed* like that before you (4) __
*came*. Anyway, I'm so glad Penny finally (5) __ *gave* you my e-mail
address.

I remember that we (6) __ *went* back to my house after school
to listen to music, but I thought we (7) __ *listened* to the Rolling
Stones, not the Beatles. Actually, I (8) __ *hated* the Beatles back
then. I don't know why—I love them now. We also (9) __ *watched*
a lot of TV, didn't we? I (10) __ *loved* those silly game shows, and I
still do!

Do you remember when we (11) __ *took* that school trip to
Washington, D.C.? It (12) __ *was* so exciting to see all of the
monuments and museums. People (13) __ *had* protests in the
capital all the time back in those days, and we (14) __ *were* so
disappointed not to see any. But of course we (15) __ *got* lost in
the city and nearly (16) __ *missed* the bus. We (17) __ *were* so
wild back then!

Oh, I (18) __ *bumped into* Dave Nelson at the mall last week.
Remember Dave? He (19) __ *was* so slim and handsome, and he
(20) __ *had* that great head of hair? Well, he's the exact opposite
of that now. But he's just as smart and funny as he (21) __ *was*
back when he (22) __ *was* the coolest kid in school.

Anyway, I'd love to get together with you and Penny. Do you have
her number? It (23) __ *was* in my phone, but I lost it when I (24) __
*changed* cell phone companies. I still can't figure out this modern
technology!

Talk to you soon!

Your old friend,
Sally Davis

P.S. It's true, I (25) __ *was* Sally Wilkinson before I got married. But
now that I've been married more than 20 years, it feels weird to
use my old name!

**2** Complete these sentences about the e-mail
with suitable words from the box. Some
words will be used more than once.

| got   weren't   used   been   would |
|---|

1. People __weren't__ used to dressing in
   bright colors before Alison came.

2. They _____ to listen to the Rolling
   Stones, not the Beatles.

3. Sally and Alison _____ watch a lot
   of TV.

4. Sally and Alison _____ used to
   getting around in Washington, D.C.

5. Dave Nelson _____ to have a lot
   of hair.

6. Sally still isn't _____ to using cell
   phones and e-mail.

7. Sally has _____ married more than
   20 years.

8. Sally _____ used to using her
   married name.

# Vocabulary

## 6 Homonyms

Use the same word to complete each pair of sentences.

1. **a.** The sun _rose_ brightly over the house this morning.

   **b.** He's very romantic. He always gives me a red _rose_ when we go on a date.

2. **a.** Look out the window, Josie—there's Daddy coming up the path! _____ to him!

   **b.** With each huge _____ , the boat was thrown about more and more, and I began to feel really sick.

3. **a.** Look, I have no idea what you're arguing about. What _____ are you trying to make?

   **b.** He couldn't speak the language, so he just used to _____ at things in stores when he was buying food.

4. **a.** Everyone has the _____ to a fair trial.

   **b.** Terrific! You got all the answers _____ on the test.

5. **a.** Wow, you look great! Is that a new _____ and tie you're wearing?

   **b.** Well, I think you should buy the pale green dress. The red one doesn't _____ you.

6. **a.** See the man with blue eyes and _____ hair? That's Jenny's husband.

   **b.** It's not _____ ! You gave him more than me!

7. **a.** Dave's OK, but he's not really my _____ of guy.

   **b.** How many words per minute can you _____ ?

8. **a.** Oh, look! Beyonce's playing at the Palladium. Can we get tickets? I'm a real _____ of hers.

   **b.** It's boiling hot. Could we turn the _____ on and get some cool air in here?

9. **a.** She'll be arriving on the 2:30 _____ . Let's go to the station and meet her.

   **b.** How many hours a week does a champion swimmer have to _____ ?

## 7 Homophones

Underline the correct word to complete each sentence.

1. I'm *board* / *bored*! I can't think of anything to do.

2. When the students entered the classroom, there were some strange words on the *board* / *bored*.

3. Stop it! You know you aren't *allowed* / *aloud* to do that!

4. Phil, can you stand up and read your story *allowed* / *aloud* to the whole class, please.

5. When we were in Alaska, we saw a *wail* / *whale*. It was really exciting to see the huge creature.

6. When she saw her bag had been stolen, she let out a *wail* / *whale* and started crying.

7. She told the police she was not sure if the person was a *mail* / *male*.

8. When they moved, they had to pick up their *mail* / *male* at the post office.

9. I need to arrange a *loan* / *lone* with my bank manager to pay off my debts.

10. The bad weather prevented us from climbing any further, but we could see one *loan* / *lone* climber on the summit.

11. They have been interviewing the whole week. They need to *higher* / *hire* someone urgently.

12. Throw the ball *higher* / *hire* or you'll never get it in the basket!

**Q** Why is Sunday the strongest day?
**A** Because all the others are week days.

**Teacher** You missed school today, Johnny, didn't you?
**Johnny** No, not at all.

# Phrasal verbs

## 8 Phrasal verbs and nouns that go together

**1** Some phrasal verbs have a strong association with certain objects: *call off a meeting* ; *work out the solution to a problem.*

Match a verb with an object. There may be more than one answer, but there is one that is best.

| | | | |
|---|---|---|---|
| 1. | **f** come up with | a. | someone you respect |
| 2. | ☐ break into | b. | someone who's done something bad |
| 3. | ☐ break off | c. | a problem, a complaint |
| 4. | ☐ tell off | d. | the other people in the group |
| 5. | ☐ bring up | e. | school before graduating |
| 6. | ☐ count on | f. | a solution to a problem |
| 7. | ☐ deal with | g. | your best friend to help you |
| 8. | ☐ drop out of | h. | children to be honest and hardworking |
| 9. | ☐ fit in with | i. | a house or an apartment to steal something |
| 10. | ☐ look up to | j. | a fact that someone might not be aware of |
| 11. | ☐ point out | k. | what I said—I didn't mean it |
| 12. | ☐ take back | l. | a relationship, an engagement |

**2** Complete the sentences with the correct forms of the phrasal verbs from Exercise 1.

1. The thieves **broke into** the warehouse and stole goods worth $20,000.

2. He _____ his elder sister because she always seemed so wise and experienced.

3. I accused you of being mean the other day. I _____ it all _____ . I'm sorry.

4. I hadn't noticed that the living room was a different color until someone _____ it _____ to me.

5. Scientists will have to _____ new methods of increasing the world's food supply.

6. She _____ Tom _____ because he was lying.

7. You have a problem with your order, ma'am? I'll get someone to _____ it for you.

8. I had a new student today. He seems very nice. I'm sure he'll _____ the rest of the class just fine.

9. Why did you _____ college after just one semester? What are you going to do now?

10. I'm running for president in the next election. I hope I can _____ your support.

11. My parents _____ me _____ to finish all the food on my plate.

12. Fred is devastated. Penny _____ their engagement last week for some reason.

# Listening

## 9 A small disagreement

**1** **CD 33** Listen to the conversation between Kathy and Eric. Mark the sentences true (✓) or false (✗).

1. An iceberg was seen near New Zealand. _____

2. The article says the sighting of the iceberg is evidence of global warming. _____

3. Eric takes global warming more seriously than Kathy does. _____

4. Kathy convinces Eric that global warming is real. _____

5. Kathy and Eric agree about the causes of global warming. _____

6. Kathy and Eric are going to do their part to reduce global warming. _____

**2** **CD 33** Listen again. Complete the lines with the correct expression.

1. _____ that could mean it's getting colder.

2. You know, _____ , it's time we did something about global warming.

3. _____ , we're running out of time.

4. _____ , all the ice is going to melt soon.

5. _____ our children will have to deal with these problems.

6. But _____ , I'm not sure there's anything we can do.

7. _____ , I'm not even sure that global warming is real.

8. _____ , how can the world be getting warmer when the weather here is so cool?

9. But _____ we don't know why this is happening.

10. Anyway, _____ we can't just sit around doing nothing.

# Pronunciation

## 10 Weak and strong forms

 **CD 34** Auxiliary verbs have weak and strong forms, depending on whether they are stressed or unstressed.

1 Sometimes the weak form is a contraction.

| | | |
|---|---|---|
| *he is* | = | *he's* |
| *she does not* | = | *she doesn't* |
| *I have not* | = | *I haven't* |

2 Sometimes the weak form is a change in the vowel sound. This is often a change to /ə/.

| | Weak | Strong |
|---|---|---|
| was | /wəz/ <br> *Was Tom there?* | /wʌz/ <br> *Yes, he was.* |
| can | /kən/ <br> *Can you swim?* | /kæn/ (can't = /kænt/) <br> *Yes, I can.* |

Some prepositions also have weak and strong vowel sounds.

| | Weak | Strong |
|---|---|---|
| to | /tə/ <br> *He's gone to Italy.* | /tu/ <br> *Where to?* |
| of | /əv/ <br> *Is he proud of it?* | /ʌv/ <br> *Kind of.* |
| at | /ət/ <br> *He arrived at two.* | /æt/ <br> *What's he looking at?* |
| for | /fər/ <br> *We talked for hours.* | /fɔr/ <br> *What's he looking for?* |
| from | /frəm/ <br> *I'm not from here.* | /frʌm/ <br> *Where are you from?* |

1 **CD 35** Circle all auxiliaries and prepositions with weak vowel sounds. Underline all those with strong vowels.

1. I don't want to see him but I'm sure you want to.

2. She isn't going to learn from this experience, but he is.

3. I've heard that you're thinking of moving from London. Are you?

4. They have dinner at seven, don't they?

5. You'll be able to get a ticket for me, won't you?

6. I have no idea who this letter's from.

7. Can't you remember who Bill used to work for?

8. We'd been looking forward to visiting them for years, then at the last minute we weren't able to.

9. Won't you sit down for a couple of minutes?

2 **CD 36** Complete the telephone conversation with the correct missing words. They are all weak forms.

A What (1) **are** you doing this weekend?

B I haven't decided yet.

A We (2) _____ going (3) _____ Vermont. (4) _____ you want (5) _____ come, too?

B I'd love to. Where (6) _____ you staying?

A We've decided (7) _____ camp. None (8) _____ us (9) _____ afford (10) _____ pay (11) _____ a hotel.

B Camping in Vermont in October? You (12) _____ be freezing cold!

A No, we won't. We (13) _____ got strong tents, lots (14) _____ warm clothes, and thick sleeping bags.

B Have you checked the weather forecast?

A (15) _____ course we have. And it (16) _____ pretty warm (17) _____ October.

B OK, then. It (18) _____ be quite an adventure!

A Excellent! I (19) _____ tell the others. They (20) _____ be delighted. We'll pick you up (21) _____ six on Friday. See you then!

# 10 Dangerous living

**Grammar:** Review of modals • Modal verbs of probability
**Vocabulary:** Physical appearance or personality
**Pronunciation:** Rhymes and limericks

## Review of modals

▶▶ **Grammar Reference 10.1**
**Student Book pp. 146–147**

### 1 Present to past

Rewrite the sentences to make them refer to the past.

1. I must mail the letters.

   <u>I had to mail the letters.</u>

2. I have to take the medication three times a day.

   _____

   _____

3. They must be away on vacation.

   _____

4. We can't see the top of the mountain.

   _____

   _____

5. He can't be a millionaire.

   _____

6. We can't shout in the classroom.

   _____

   _____

7. He won't go to bed.

   _____

8. That must be Greg on the phone.

   _____

9. You should be more careful.

   _____

10. You could do the dishes for a change.

    _____

    _____

## Modal verbs of probability

### 2 How certain?

**1** Decide on the degree of certainty in these sentences. Put two checks (✓✓) next to the sentences if the idea expressed is certain. Put one check (✓) if it is less certain.

1. ✓✓ You must have seen him at the theater. I know he was there.
2. ✓ The dog is really dirty. He might have swum in the lake.
3. ☐ He can't have been telling the truth.
4. ☐ He might have left a message on your cell phone.
5. ☐ I don't know where she is. She may have gone shopping.
6. ☐ She must have been very upset when you told her the news.
7. ☐ They're not answering the phone. They must have gone away already.
8. ☐ I don't see their car. They can't have come back yet.
9. ☐ It's six o'clock. Tom should have gone home by now.
10. ☐ Matthew isn't here. He might have thought you weren't coming and gone to the movies by himself.
11. ☐ I could have canceled the meeting if I'd known earlier!
12. ☐ Joe will be back soon. It's Friday. He must have gone to the gym after work.

**2** Make sentences combining the lines in the box.

| If I go to India, I<br>If I went to India, I<br>If I'd gone to India, I | can<br>will<br>may<br>might<br>would<br>could | see the Taj Mahal.<br><br>have seen the Taj Mahal. |
|---|---|---|

1. <u>If I go to India, I can see the Taj Mahal.</u>
2. _____
3. _____
4. _____
5. _____
6. _____
7. _____
8. _____
9. _____

## 3 Past probability

**1** Write sentences for the situations below, using the information in the box.

| He She They | must have can't have might have | cut it gone lost arrived home gotten engaged had been doing been making | a cake. a party last night. to Calvin. something bad. for a long time. without me. by now. my number. |
|---|---|---|---|

1. Stella's wearing a beautiful diamond ring.

   <u>**She must have gotten engaged to Calvin.**</u>

2. Look at the length of the grass in Henry's yard.

   _____

   _____

3. The children ran away laughing and giggling.

   _____

   _____

4. There's flour on Grandma's nose.

   _____

   _____

5. Paulo and Gina said they'd wait for me, but I can't see them.

   _____

   _____

6. Karl's apartment is so clean and neat.

   _____

   _____

7. It's after midnight. Henry and Sally left a while ago.

   _____

   _____

8. I don't know why Sara didn't call.

   _____

   _____

**2** Write sentences for the situations below using the information in the box.

| It They | must have been can't have been | watered washed hit blown down repaired | by the wind. by a stone. properly. while we were away. with something red. |
|---|---|---|---|

1. A tree has fallen across the road.

   <u>**It must have been blown down by the wind.**</u>

2. My white jeans have turned pink!

   _____

   _____

3. My TV has broken, and I just had it fixed last week.

   _____

   _____

4. All the flowers in the garden have died.

   _____

   _____

5. The car windshield is broken.

   _____

   _____

## 4 Past modals of deduction

Complete the conversations with the correct form of the verbs in parentheses.

1.  A  I wonder how the thief got into our apartment.
    B  He (1) <u>could have used</u> (could / use) the fire escape, or he (2) _____ (might / climb up) that tree.
    A  Well, he (3) _____ (should not / bother). There's nothing to steal!

2.  A  Bill told me that he'd spent $2,000 on a birthday present for his girlfriend, but he (4) _____ (must / joke). Surely he (5) _____ (can not / spend) that much.
    B  I think you (6) _____ (might / mishear) him!

3.  A  It's 3:30. Mom and Dad's plane landed over an hour ago. They (7) _____ (should / call)!
    B  They (8) _____ (may / be delayed). No, look! They're driving up now.

4.  A  You're very sunburned. You (9) _____ (would not / burn) if you had used your SPF 30 sunscreen.
    B  I (10) _____ (must / fall) asleep. And I (11) _____ (can not / put on) enough sunscreen. Ouch!

## 5 Past modals – various uses

<u>Underline</u> the correct answer.

1.  I'm sorry. I *shouldn't have* / *couldn't have* told Tom what you said about him.

2.  A  Where's the dog?
    B  Don't know. Dad *may have* / *must have* taken him for a walk.
    A  No. I remember. It's Tuesday, isn't it? Mom *should have* / *must have* taken him to the vet.

3.  A  Are Pat and Jan definitely coming? I'*d have* / *might have* thought they'd have arrived by now.
    B  They *should have* / *could have* been held up by traffic.
    A  Or they *might have* / *couldn't have* gotten in an accident!
    B  Don't be silly. Anyway, we'*d have* / *must have* heard by now if something like that had happened.
    A  Well, I *shouldn't have* / *can't have* prepared lunch so early. And I think they *should have* / *may have* called if they knew they were going to be late.

4.  A  Who was that man?
    B  He *can't have* / *must have* been a friend of Terry's. He was asking if I'd seen her.

# Water, Water Everywhere!

The recent discovery of ice on the Moon means three places are now known to have some form of water: the Moon, Mars, and, of course, Earth. It also raises lots of questions. Space scientist DR. CLEO ALLAN offers some answers.

## 6 Water, Water Everywhere!

1  Read the article and choose the correct answers.

1.  The places known to have water are
    a. ☐ the Earth and the Moon.
    b. ☐ the Earth, the Moon, and Mars.

2.  Astronauts didn't find water on the Moon 40 years ago because
    a. ☐ they weren't looking for it.
    b. ☐ they were looking for it in the wrong place.

3.  Scientists think that Mars
    a. ☐ couldn't ever have supported life.
    b. ☐ may once have supported life.

2  Complete the article by putting the verbs in parentheses in the past. You will need to use a passive form once.

**Why did it take so long to discover water on the Moon? Didn't people go there more than 40 years ago?**

Yes, but they didn't go to this particular part of the Moon, near its south pole. This area almost never receives sunlight, so any water there would stay frozen. I suppose they (1) _____ (can / go) there 40 years ago, but it (2) _____ (will / be) expensive and dangerous. Anyway, no one expected to find water on the Moon in 1969. They assumed it was a "dead" place, so in their minds there (3) _____ (can not / be) any water on it.

**So how was water discovered this time?**

Scientists crashed a space probe into the moon, while another probe took measurements of the dust that flew out of the impact. There were at least 25 gallons of frozen water in the dust, and there (4) _____ (may / be) even more than that. Before the crash, the water (5) _____ (may / stay) frozen under the surface for over a billion years.

**How did water get on the Moon, anyway?**

No one knows for sure. It (6) _____ (can / come) from comets, which are just big chunks of ice and dust flying through space. The water also (7) _____ (can / appear) from a source inside the Moon. More research is needed.

**Does this mean there was once life on the Moon?**

No, or at least not life as we know it. The Moon has no air to breathe, so scientists think it (8) _____ ever _____ (can not / support) life.

Mars, on the other hand, is a different story. There (9) _____ (may / be) a thicker atmosphere on Mars in the past, so perhaps something (10) _____ (can / live) there millions of years ago. Also, a meteorite was found on Earth in the 1990s that (11) _____ (must / come) from Mars because it is made of the same kind of rock. And interesting "micro-fossils" were found on this meteor that (12) _____ (may / be left) by microscopic life forms. But there is still a lot of debate about that. ∎

# Listening

## 7 Getting along

1 **CD 37** Listen to the conversation between Alicia and Beth. Answer the questions.

  1. Why is there conflict at home?

  2. What did Beth's sister say that hurt her parents?

  3. How are things at home now?

2 **CD 37** Listen again. Complete the sentences with a body idiom.

  1. They had a big _____ last weekend, and that helped.

  2. I've had my _____ with setting everything up.

  3. My sister's having to_____ that she's the only child left at home now.

  4. She tried, but her _____ wasn't in it.

  5. She has a very good _____ , doesn't she?

  6. She's always had a bit of a _____ , hasn't she?

  7. Wow, you must be _____ !

  8. . . . my parents are going to _____ with running it.

# Vocabulary

## 8 Physical appearance or personality?

1 Write these adjectives in the correct columns.

| | | |
|---|---|---|
| moody | bigheaded | brainy |
| graceful | wrinkled | quick-thinking |
| skinny | nosy | bald |
| well-built | narrow-minded | affectionate |
| smart | curly | hard-hearted |

| Physical appearance | Personality |
|---|---|
| graceful | moody |
| | |

2 Complete the sentences with the correct forms of the verbs in the box.

| elbow eye foot hand head shoulder thumb |
|---|

  1. The teacher _**handed**_____ out the tests and told the class to begin writing.

  2. I managed to _____ my way to the front of the crowd, so I got a good view of the parade.

  3. I haven't read the magazine yet. I just _____ through it to see if there were any interesting pictures.

  4. We all _____ the new student with curiosity. We were eager to see what she was like.

  5. They ordered the most expensive things on the menu because they knew that I _____ the bill.

  6. In the final seconds of the game, Benson _____ the ball into the goal, making it 1–1.

  7. I'd hate to be president. I don't think I could _____ the responsibility of making so many important decisions.

# Prepositions

## 9 Verb + preposition

Complete the sentences with a verb in its correct form and a preposition.

| Verbs | | Prepositions | |
|---|---|---|---|
| thank | forgive | into | of |
| accuse | hide | at | on |
| trick | hold | for | to |
| congratulate | inherit | from | |
| shout | model | | |
| invite | remind | | |

1. He **thanked** the nurse **for** all her help.

2. You _____ me so much _____ your father. You look just like him.

3. Everyone _____ me _____ passing my driver's test on the fourth try.

4. My teenage daughter always _____ herself _____ her latest pop idol. She just bought herself a leather jacket, just like him.

5. Don't _____ the truth _____ me. I want to know everything.

6. He picked up the crying baby and _____ her tightly _____ his chest.

7. We've _____ 300 guests _____ our wedding.

8. I think that TV ads _____ people _____ buying things that they don't really need.

9. I didn't _____ a penny _____ my great uncle when he died.

10. She was so rude! She _____ _____ him in front of everybody.

11. How can I ever _____ him _____ telling me all those lies?

12. My employers _____ me _____ stealing, which I strongly denied.

# Pronunciation

## 10 Rhymes and limericks

1 **CD 38** Make rhyming pairs with the words from the box.

| | | | | | |
|---|---|---|---|---|---|
| ~~good~~ | chief | bought | deaf | fool | put |
| mud | height | lose | knew | knows | grieve |
| reign | nude | said | pour | weight | wool |

1. should /ʊd/ **good**
2. bread /ɛd/ _____
3. choose /uz/ _____
4. toes /oʊz/ _____
5. hate /eɪt/ _____
6. tight /aɪt/ _____
7. full /ʊl/ _____
8. pool /ul/ _____
9. blood /ʌd/ _____
10. food /ud/ _____
11. leaf /if/ _____
12. taught /ɔt/ _____
13. chef /ɛf/ _____
14. through /u/ _____
15. wore /ɔ/ _____
16. brain /eɪn/ _____
17. leave /iv/ _____
18. foot /ʊt/ _____

2 **CD 39** Limericks are short humorous poems with five lines and a distinctive rhythm. The lines rhyme AABBA. Complete the lines with the words from the box.

| | | | |
|---|---|---|---|
| chalk | them (2×) | ~~Twickenham~~ | walk |

## The Lady from Twickenham

There was a young lady
  from (1) **Twickenham**

Whose shoes were too tight
  to walk quick in (2) _____.

She came back from a (3) _____

Looking whiter than (4) _____.

And she took them both off
  and was sick in (5) _____.

# 11 In your dreams

**Grammar:** Real or unreal time? •
Wishes and regrets
**Vocabulary:** Similar words,
different meanings
**Pronunciation:** Ways of pronouncing *ea*

## Real time or unreal time?

▶▶ **Grammar Reference 11.1 Student Book p. 147**

### 1 Real or hypothetical past?

1 These sentences all have verbs in the Past Simple. Put a check (✓) next to those that refer to real past time. What do the others refer to?

1. ✓ Did you see Lorenzo when you were in Italy?
2. ☐ I wish I worked outdoors.
3. ☐ If you took the medication, you wouldn't cough so much.
4. ☐ When we lived in London we'd always travel by bus.
5. ☐ I'd rather we lived in a small country town.
6. ☐ It's time we had a new car.
7. ☐ If only you were always as happy as you are today.
8. ☐ Why didn't you come to the party?

2 These sentences all have verbs in the Past Perfect. Put a check (✓) next to those that express reality.

1. ✓ She asked me if I had known him for a long time.
2. ☐ I wish I'd said that.
3. ☐ If I hadn't been so nervous, I would have passed the exam.
4. ☐ If only you'd arrived five minutes earlier.
5. ☐ I woke up and realized it had all been a terrible dream.
6. ☐ What if they hadn't agreed to give you a pay raise?
7. ☐ She told me she'd been given a car for her birthday.

3 Complete the sentences below with an auxiliary verb which expresses reality.

1. I wish you didn't bite your nails, but you **_do_** .
2. I wish I earned more, but I _____ .
3. I should have listened to their advice, but I _____.
4. If only I could speak Korean, but I _____ .
5. If only he weren't so selfish, but he _____ .
6. I wish my car would start, but it _____ .
7. I wish you didn't argue all the time, but you _____ .
8. If only I hadn't been fired, but I _____ .
9. I wish I had my own apartment, but I _____ .

## Wishes and regrets

### 2 Present and past wishes

1 Use the words from the columns to make as many correct and logical sentences as you can.

| I wish | you<br>I | were<br>could<br>would<br>had | come.<br>rich. |
|--------|----------|-------------------------------|----------------|

_____

_____

_____

_____

_____

_____

2 Underline the correct alternative in the following sentences. Sometimes two are possible.

1. I really wish I *can* / *could* / *was able to* speak another language.
2. I wish it *wasn't* / *wouldn't be* / *isn't* so cold. I hate the winter.
3. It's time we *take* / *took* / *have taken* a vacation.
4. Our vacation was a disaster. I'd rather we *didn't go* / *hadn't gone* / *weren't going*.
5. The party was so good after you left. You should *stay* / *had stayed* / *have stayed* longer.
6. I wish you *don't speak* / *didn't speak* / *wouldn't speak* so quickly. I can't follow you.
7. What were you doing on that wall? Supposing you *had had* / *would have* / *hadn't had* an accident?
8. She'd rather her grandchildren *live* / *lived* / *had lived* nearer. Then she could see them more often.

## 3 Expressions of regret

**1** Rewrite the sentences so that they have similar meanings. Use the words in parentheses.

1. I'm sorry I didn't invite him to the party. (wish)

   <u>I wish I had invited him to the party.</u>

2. Why weren't you watching the road? (should)

   _____

3. I regret saying that to her. (If only)

   _____

4. I shouldn't have hit him. (wish)

   _____

5. I don't want you to tell her. ('d rather)

   _____

6. I don't like it when Lucy stays out so late. (wish)

   _____

7. I regret I didn't work harder for the tests. (should)

   _____

**2** Write sentences to express these people's wishes and regrets. Use the expressions in parentheses from Exercise 1.

1. <u>I wish I had a larger car.</u>   2. _____

   _____

3. _____   4. _____

   _____

5. _____   6. _____

   _____

## 4 What I wish I'd known…

Complete each paragraph in the article with words from the preceeding box.

# What I wish I'd known when I was 20

| had | would | should | ~~wish~~ | only | could | have |

**Stephanie Lewis,** 45, MOTHER AND TEACHER

I (1) <u>wish</u> I hadn't given my mother such a hard time at that age. If (2) _____ she (3) _____ have lived to see the trouble my own kids give me! I'm sure she (4) _____ have said, "I told you so!" I (5) _____ have behaved better as a kid. If I (6) _____, maybe I'd (7) _____ better luck with my own kids!

| got | would | hadn't | have | finished | had | unless |

**Don Wilson**, 62, SALES MANAGER

I wish I (8) _____ spent more time studying when I was in my teens and twenties. Even though I (9) _____ college and (10) _____ a good job, I didn't learn anything. I (11) _____ go to every party in college, but I never went to class (12) _____ I really had to. If I (13) _____ wasted the chance to learn, I could (14) _____ gone to graduate school and done something really meaningful. Now I'm stuck in a boring career.

| went | 'd | didn't | could | hadn't | wasn't |

**April Wong**, 31, ARTIST

I (15) _____ always loved art when I was a kid, but my parents pushed me to study law. I wish I (16) _____ listened to them. Instead, I (17) _____ to law school for two years, then I quit to follow my dream to be an artist. But if only I (18) _____ have all that debt from law school! I (19) _____ produce more art if I (20) _____ working part time to pay off my student loans.

# Third conditional

## 5 My first crash

**1** **CD 40** Read the article and complete the story with the words in the box.

| | |
|---|---|
| would have ended up | was coming around |
| came to a sudden stop | It was boring |
| we were having | ~~used to work~~ |
| could see the face | didn't ever talk |
| I could do | was annoyed |

# My first crash

**by Philippa Forrester**

"When I was a poor student I (1) **used to work** during my vacation for spare cash. One year I spent six weeks in the accounts department of a local firm. (2) _____ , but there was this handsome guy working there called John, and I had a crush on him.

A friend of mine used to drive me to an out-of-town aerobics class after work, and I remember on this particular day (3) _____ a girlie talk about my crush. She was obviously fascinated by my tale of infatuation because she was momentarily distracted from looking at the road, and she went around the corner a little too wide and crossed to the other side of the road.

Unfortunately for us, another car (4) _____ the corner in the opposite direction. But what made it all particularly bizarre was that I (5) _____ of the other driver—it was John from accounts!

I can remember starting to blush as we sailed straight into the side of his car. We (6) _____ with the sound of breaking glass from our headlights, and we got out, embarrassed, wearing our Lycra aerobics outfits.

What a ridiculous coincidence it all was. But I was secretly thrilled—all (7) _____ was stand with my mouth open and say, "Oh, look, it's John from accounts!" My friend exchanged insurance details with him and that was that. In a fairy tale, John and I (8) _____ making a date, getting

**2** Now complete the sentences about the story using the verbs in parentheses in the third conditional. Careful! Sometimes you need to use the continuous form.

1. If Phillipa **hadn't been** (be) a poor student, she **wouldn't have been working** (work) for six weeks in a local firm.

2. She _____ (meet) John if she _____ (work) in the accounts department.

3. She _____ (can / go) to the aerobics classes if her friend _____ (pick her up) in her car.

4. If she _____ (talk) to her friend, her friend _____ (cross) to the other side of the road.

5. If there _____ (be) a car coming in the opposite direction, they _____ (crash).

6. She _____ (blush) if John from accounts _____ (be) in the other car.

7. If she _____ (go) to an aerobics class, she _____ (wear) her Lycra outfit.

8. John _____ (might / continue) talking to her if she _____ (crash) into him.

together, and driving off happily ever after. But he probably thought I looked like an idiot in my Lycra outfit because he (9) _____ to me after that.

My friend's car wasn't too badly damaged, but she (10) _____ that it was her fault. However, she also saw the funny side—that a crush had turned into a crash.

**3** Rearrange the words to make excuses in the third conditional.

1. wouldn't / been / if / sick / hadn't / shellfish / had / I / I / have / the

   _____

   _____

2. called / had / had / if / you / have / time / would / I / the / I

   _____

   _____

3. if / known / had / I / the / washable / wasn't / wouldn't / I / bought / have / it / sweater

   _____

   _____

4. if / it / own / my / eyes / seen / with / hadn't / I / wouldn't / believed / I / have / it

   _____

   _____

**4** Complete the second sentence to express the excuse in a different way.

1. I didn't know you were in town. I didn't call you.

   **If I'd known you were in town, I could / would have called you.**

2. I didn't send you a postcard because I didn't know your address.

   If I _____

   _____ a postcard.

3. I didn't remember when your birthday was. That's why I didn't buy you a present.

   If _____

   _____ .

4. I'm sorry I'm late. I forgot to set my alarm clock.

   If _____

   _____ .

5. I broke the speed limit because I was taking my wife to the hospital.

   If _____

   _____ .

# All conditionals

## 6 Review of all conditionals

Put the verbs in parentheses in the correct tense to form either the first, second, third, or zero conditional. There are also some examples of mixed conditionals.

1. If I still _feel_____ (feel) sick, I **won't go**_____ (not go) on vacation next weekend.

2. You make such delicious chocolate cakes! If you _____ (sell) them, you _____ (make) a fortune.

3. Hello, Liz. Are you still looking for Pat? If I _____ (see) her, I _____ (tell) her you want to speak to her.

4. If Alice _____ (not go) to Harvard, she _____ (not met) her husband, Andrew.

5. **A** Does she love him?

   **B** Of course. If she _____ (not love) him, she _____ (not marry) him today.

6. If you _____ (buy) two apples, you _____ (get) one free.

7. **A** What _____ you _____ (do) if you _____ (see) a ghost?

   **B** I _____ (run) away!

8. We're lost. If we _____ (bring) the map with us, we _____ (know) where we are.

9. You were very lucky to catch the fire in time. If you _____ (not have) a smoke alarm installed, the house _____ (burn down).

10. You were very rude to Max. If I _____ (be) you, I _____ (apologize).

11. Jeff is allergic to cheese. If he _____ (eat) cheese, he _____ (get) an awful rash.

12. We've run out of gas. If you _____ (listen) to me sometimes instead of being so stubborn, you _____ (hear) me saying that we were running low. Then we _____ (not be) stuck here.

# Ways of introducing conditionals

1 Conditionals can be introduced in a variety of ways other than with *if*.

**unless**
*Unless* means "except if. "

> *We'll go swimming **unless** it rains.*

> ***Unless** there's a strike, I'll be at work tomorrow.*

**in case**
*In case* means the first action is a precaution: it happens because the second action *might* happen. Compare these two sentences:

> *I'll take my umbrella **in case** it rains.* (I plan to take my umbrella.)

> *I'll take my umbrella **if** it rains.* (I don't plan to take my umbrella if I don't have to.)

**Supposing… / Suppose… / Imagine…**
These mean the same as "Imagine if…" or "What if…?" The condition is more improbable, so they are more often found in second and third conditionals. They are usually followed by questions and come at the beginning of a sentence.

> ***Supposing** you could go on vacation tomorrow, where would you go?*

> ***Imagine** you were rich, what would you buy?*

2 In more formal styles *if* can be dropped and the auxiliary verb inverted.

> ***Were** you to **question** me about the matter, I would deny all knowledge.*

> ***Had** I **known** that he was a journalist, I would have said nothing.*

> ***Should** the meeting **last** longer than expected, I'll have to cancel my dinner engagement.*

"He refuses to come down unless you agree to all of his demands."

## 7 Words other than *if*

1 Underline the correct alternative.

1. *In case / Imagine* there were no more wars. Wouldn't that be wonderful?
2. I'm going to take a cushion to the concert *in case / unless* the seats are hard.
3. We'll miss the beginning of the movie *in case / unless* you hurry.
4. *Unless / In case* you behave yourself, you can't come to the party with us.
5. *Suppose / Should* you got lost, what would you do?
6. I'll take a book *in case / unless* I'm bored on the trip.
7. *Had / Supposing* I understood the problem, I'd have done something about it.
8. *Should / In case* you fail to pay this bill, court action will be taken.

2 Rewrite the sentences below using the words in parentheses.

1. I won't come if they don't invite me. (unless)

   I won't come unless they invite me.

2. What would you do if he left you? (supposing)

3. If you had learned to play tennis, would you have been a champion by now? (suppose)

4. We're going to install a smoke alarm. There may be a fire. (in case)

5. She won't get that job if she doesn't learn to speak French. (unless)

6. If the lifeguard hadn't been there, what would have happened? (imagine)

7. I won't go out this evening. Paul might call. (in case)

8. I'll be at my desk until 6:00 if you need to speak to me about the matter. (should)

# Vocabulary

## 8 Similar words, different meanings

These adjective pairs are easy to confuse. Complete the sentences with the correct adjectives.

| unreadable | illegible |
|---|---|

1. I couldn't figure out who the letter was from. The signature was completely _____ .

2. I know Shakespeare is very popular, but I find him totally _____ .

| childish | childlike |
|---|---|

3. Sarah is so _____ . She's always having temper tantrums.

4. It was wonderful to watch the lambs playing. I got such _____ pleasure from it.

| sensible | sensitive |
|---|---|

5. Sophie is extremely _____ right now. Anything you say upsets her.

6. Karen is not a very _____ person. She wore high-heeled shoes for our four-mile walk.

| true | truthful |
|---|---|

7. I've never known her to tell a lie. She's a very _____ person.

8. I can never watch sad movies that are based on a _____ story. They always make me cry.

| intolerable | intolerant |
|---|---|

9. Susan is so _____ of other people. She never accepts anyone else's opinion, and she always thinks she knows best.

10. I find Mark's behavior _____ . It's unfair to be so selfish.

| economic | economical |
|---|---|

11. We're having an _____ crisis right now. James has lost his job, and I don't know how we are going to pay the mortgage.

12. It's much more _____ to drive slowly. You get more miles for your money.

# Phrasal verbs

## 9 Nouns from phrasal verbs

 There are many nouns formed from phrasal verbs. Sometimes the verb comes first, sometimes second.

| *make*up | *down*fall | *up*bringing |
|---|---|---|
| *draw*back | *out*break | *take*out |

Complete these sentences with the nouns in the box.

| outcome | breakthrough | outbreak | takeout |
|---|---|---|---|
| checkup | ~~breakdown~~ | comeback | feedback |
| outlook | downfall | | |

1. The __breakdown__ of communication between management and workers means the strike will continue.

2. His pop career has suffered recently, but now with a new album and a world tour, he's trying to make a _____ .

3. I go to the dentist twice a year for a _____ .

4. The _____ of the election is that the Republican party has a majority.

5. The weather should be fine over the next few days, and the _____ for the weekend is warm and sunny.

6. There has been an _____ of food poisoning as a result of people eating poorly-cooked chicken.

7. There has been a significant _____ in the search to find a cure for the common cold.

8. Producers ask customers to complete questionnaires because they need _____ to improve their products.

9. We're having Chinese _____ for supper.

10. He used to be a highly successful pop star, but too many problems with his manager was his _____ .

# Listening

## 10 What a pain!

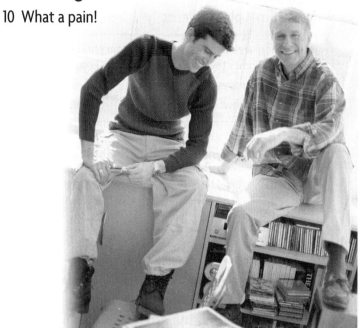

**1** **CD 41** Listen and answer the questions.

1. What's Mark trying to do?
2. What two things is he having trouble with?
3. What does Greg think is the problem?
4. Why does Mark get upset?
5. Who finds the solution and how?

**2** **CD 41** Listen again and match these expressions with *if*.

| | |
|---|---|
| 1. I haven't made much progress, | a. they'll just have to give you your money back. |
| 2. If you've got a minute, | b. if any. |
| 3. If worse comes to worst, | c. that'd be great. |
| 4. Here are your missing parts, | d. you might just be finished by then! |
| 5. If all goes well from now on, | e. if I'm not mistaken. |

**3** Who says these things? Write **M** (Mark) or **G** (Greg).

1. It's turning into a nightmare already. **M** .
2. What a pain! _____
3. Don't ask me! _____
4. I can't believe it! _____
5. You've got to be kidding! _____
6. It's just that I'm sick of the whole thing already. _____
7. This sort of thing drives me crazy, too. _____
8. I could kick myself! _____

# Pronunciation

## 11 Ways of pronouncing *ea*

**1** There are different ways of pronouncing the letters *ea*. Look at the examples in the columns below.

| /ɛ/ | /i/ | /ɪ/ |
|---|---|---|
| bread | meat | fear |
| | /eɪ/ | /ə/ |
| | break | learn |

**2** **CD 42** Put these words into the correct column above according to the pronunciation of *ea*.

| | | |
|---|---|---|
| dear | tear (n) | tear (v) |
| scream | steak | breath |
| breathe | breadth | hear |
| thread | cheat | clear |
| deaf | death | earth |
| beast | beard | pearl |
| heal | health | great |
| gear | jealous | lead (v) |
| lead (n) | leap | leaped |
| meant | reason | search |
| beat | weary | weapon |

# 12 It's never too late.

**Grammar:** Articles • Determiners • Demonstratives
**Vocabulary:** *be* and *have*
**Pronunciation:** Nouns and verbs • Emphasis in speaking

## Articles

▶▶ **Grammar Reference 12.1 Student Book p. 148**

### 1 *a*, *the*, or zero article?

1 Complete the sentences with *a*, *the*, or nothing (the zero article).

1. Excuse me! Is there **a** bank near here?

2. **A** I don't have any money.
   **B** I'm going to ____ bank. I'll get you some.

3. Has ____ mail carrier already been here this morning?

4. My brother works as ____ mail carrier.

5. We've seen a house we want to move to. It has ____ views of fields, and there's ____ great yard in ____ back.

6. **A** Where's Nick?
   **B** In ____ backyard.

7. I bought ____ cat to help get rid of ____ mice.

8. Jonathan gave to ____ Humane Society because he wants to help ____ cats.

9. We went out for ____ dinner last night. ____ food was excellent. I don't usually like ____ Italian food, but ____ pasta was superb.

2 Complete the newspaper article with *a*, *an*, *the*, *her*, or nothing.

## It's never too early

Ghita, 8, passes college-level exam in computer science

(1) **An** eight-year-old girl became one of (2) ____ youngest students ever to pass (3) ____ college-level exam in computer science in this country.

Ghita Subramarian's (4) ____ achievement was also (5) ____ latest achievement for (6) ____ school run from two rooms of (7) ____ house in Seattle.

Ghita managed to pass the test by studying for several evenings (8) ____ week at (9) ____ nearby Ellesmere School for Young Children.

"I think (10) ____ computers are easy, but I thought (11) ____ test was pretty hard," Ghita said. She praised (12) ____ teacher, James Nolan,

(13) ____ founder and principal of Ellesmere School. "He is (14) ____ nice teacher—he tells (15) ____ jokes!"

Dr. Nolan commented: "You must have (16) ____ faith in children. They can make (17) ____ paper planes one minute and write (18) ____ computer program (19) ____ next. (20) ____ students at my school aren't prodigies—they are just interested and motivated. They are (21) ____ example of what (22) ____ rest of (23) ____ country could be doing.

As far as I'm concerned, students who go to college are the 'senior citizens' of (24) ____ academic world, having passed their mental peak."

# Determiners

▶▶ Grammar Reference 12.1 Student Book p. 154

## 2 *all* and *every*

**1** Underline the correct answer.

1. Anna is such a show-off. She thinks she knows *all / everything*.

2. My driver's test was a complete disaster. *All / Everything* went wrong.

3. Grace didn't say where she was going. *All / Everything* she said was that she was going out.

4. *All / Every* child in the class failed the test.

5. *All / Everything* I want for my birthday is to lie in bed until noon.

6. I'm starving. *All / Everything* I've eaten today is a bag of potato chips.

7. I really don't get along with my new boss. I disagree with *all / everything* she says.

8. I can't go higher than $5,000 for the car. That's *everything / all* I can afford.

9. Marion couldn't believe her luck. *All / Every* topic she had reviewed the night before came up on the test.

10. The play was so boring that *all / everybody* fell asleep.

**2** Underline the correct answer.

1. My two daughters are *each / both* good at languages, but *none / neither* of them can do math at all.

2. I take a shower *every / each* day.

3. I have *any / no* idea how I spend all my money. At the end of *every / either* month, it's all gone.

4. I know *every / each* word of his songs by heart.

5. There are 15 rooms in this hotel. *Each / Every* room is a little different.

6. You can have *either / each* an orange or an apple, but you can't have *either / both*.

7. **A** Tea or coffee?
   **B** *Either / Neither*, thanks. I have to run.

8. **A** Orange or apple juice?
   **B** *Either / Neither*, whichever is open.

9. I know *either / both* Robert and his brother, but I don't like *both / either* of them.

10. I have four brothers. *Every / Each* of us is different.

# Demonstratives

## 3 *this*, *that*, *these*, *those*

Fill in the blanks with *this*, *that*, *these*, or *those*.

1. __These__ shoes are killing me. I can't wait to take them off.

2. (On the phone) Hello. _____ is Beth. Can I speak to Clare?

3. _____ was a wonderful musical, wasn't it?

4. I knew Jenny from college. In _____ days she had long blond hair.

5. **A** Anything else?
   **B** No, _____ 's all for today, thanks.

6. What was _____ noise? Didn't you hear it?

7. I can't get _____ ring off my finger. It's stuck.

8. You just can't get good cars _____ days.

9. Come here and clean up _____ mess right now!

10. Listen to _____. It says in the paper that life's been found on Mars.

11. Did you ever hear from _____ girl you met in Prague last year?

12. I was walking home last night when _____ guy came up to me and asked me the time.

13. **A** I got a parking ticket today.
    **B** _____ 'll teach you a lesson.

14. Who were _____ people you were talking to last night?

15. Well, _____ 'll be $5.50, please.

# Review of articles, determiners, and demonstratives

## 4 Personal column

Complete the article with the words and expressions in the boxes.

Personal column

# She's a world-traveling, windsurfing retiree who refuses to act her age

### BY SIMON MARTIN

| every one | her | all of the | the | a | a great deal of |
|---|---|---|---|---|---|

ELSIE MORECAMBE looks up at (1) __all of the__ large gray clouds coming quickly over (2) _____ horizon. "I'll go just (3) _____ last time," she says, jumping onto (4) _____ windsurfing board and speeding off over rough waves.

Back on dry land, (5) _____ group of elderly people watches (6) _____ move she makes with (7) _____ admiration.

| enough | an | the | her | a lot of | a great deal |
|---|---|---|---|---|---|

Four years ago, at 70, looking (8) _____ younger than her years, Elsie formed (9) _____ organization called Age Well. "It isn't (10) _____ to tell people—you have to show them," she says, dragging (11) _____ board ashore to (12) _____ backslapping and praise from (13) _____ group.

| all | her | everything | no | those | their |
|---|---|---|---|---|---|

This is all part of (14) _____ campaign to show that people of (15) _____ ages can achieve (16) _____ they want to do, if they really want to do it. "It struck me that (17) _____ friends of mine who had (18) _____ job to go to anymore, and who kept complaining about (19) _____ boring and meaningless lives, didn't have to live like that," she commented.

| the (× 2) | her (× 2) | this | most | a | several |
|---|---|---|---|---|---|

Elsie has been windsurfing (20) _____ summer months for the last six years, ever since (21) _____ son told her that she was far too old to attempt it. Then she went on (22) _____ solo six-month world trip to Mexico, Thailand, and New Zealand.

Over the last four years she has organized and led (23) _____ groups on trips to Ireland, Israel, and Greece.

So far (24) _____ year she has been walking in (25) _____ Pyrénées, touring on (26) _____ bicycle, and canoeing.

"(27) _____ secret to life is ignoring how old you are," Elsie says.

# Nouns in groups

1 There are three main ways that we can put nouns together.

| noun + noun | noun + 's + noun |
|---|---|
| *post office* | *my wife's sister* |
| *headache* | *the doctor's office* |
| *face-lift* | *the men's room* |

noun + preposition + noun

*the end of the game*
*a story about compassion*
*the arrival of the police*

2 Sometimes more than one structure can be used.

*the president's arrival*
*the arrival of the president*

*the floor of the living room*
*the living room floor*

*the car door handle*
*the handle on the car door*

But usually only one pattern is possible.

*the back of the car*
NOT ~~the car back~~   ~~the car's back~~

3 Sometimes there is a change in meaning.

*the cat's food* = the food that belongs to one particular cat

The mice have eaten the cat's food.

*cat food* = food for cats in general

Can you buy some more cat food when you go out?

4 We use the noun + noun pattern (compound nouns) for everyday established combinations. We talk about a war movie, a horror movie, but not ~~a horse movie~~. Here we usually prefer the pattern with a preposition – a movie about horses.

## 5 Combining nouns

Combine the words in parentheses to fill in the blanks.

1. Your coat's on the <u>back of the chair</u> (back, chair).

2. You've just spilled the _____ (milk, cat).

3. Can you buy some _____ (paper, toilet)? We've run out.

4. I never listened to my _____ (advice, parents).

5. Can you buy a _____ (water, bottle)?

6. What did that _____ (road, sign) say? Did you see it?

7. Are there any _____ (paper, towels) in the kitchen? I just spilled something.

8. The _____ (president, duties) include entertaining heads of state.

9. The _____ (my shoe, heel) has come off.

10. Can I borrow your _____ (brush, hair)?

11. What happened at the _____ (movie, end)?

12. Here is _____ (today, news).

13. Where is the nearest _____ (subway, station)?

14. It's _____ (anniversary, my parents, wedding) next week.

15. The _____ (company, success) is due to its efficiency.

16. I've got a _____ (week, vacation) next month.

17. The _____ (government, economic policy) is confusing.

18. The annual _____ (rate, inflation) is about 4 percent.

19. It's such a mess in here. There are dirty _____ (coffee, cups) everywhere.

20. Do you want a _____ (coffee, cup)?

# Vocabulary

## 6 be and have

**1** Match the words and expressions with *be* or *have*. Put a check (✓) in the correct column.

| be | | have |
|:---:|---|:---:|
| ✓ | fed up with sb/sth | |
| | the right to do sth | ✓ |
| | the nerve to do sth | |
| | on the safe side | |
| | in touch with sb | |
| | a talk with sb | |
| | no point in doing sth | |
| | on one's mind | |
| | up to date | |
| | no chance of doing sth | |

**2** Complete the sentences with some of the expressions from Exercise 1 in the correct form.

1. My job is so boring. I **'m** really **fed up with** it.

2. If you don't like your meal, you _____ complain to the manager.

3. Thank you for your interview, Ms. Clarke. We _____ you as soon as we've made a decision about the job.

4. I can't stop thinking about my ex-girlfriend. She _____ always _____ .

5. Mrs. Bennett! Can I _____ you for a minute? It's about your son Ben.

6. Jack was so rude! He _____ tell me that this dress didn't suit me!

7. I got extra travel insurance just in case. I always like _____ .

8. Well, I'll apply for the manager's job, but I know I _____ getting it.

9. Wait here. If you don't like heights, there _____ climbing up the tower with us.

10. I got an e-mail from my old friend Suzanne the other day. I _____ her for 20 years now!

# Prepositions review

## 7 Noun and preposition

Complete the sentences with a preposition or a combination of prepositions.

1. After running up the stairs, I was **out of** breath.

2. You make some silly mistakes, but _____ general your work has been good.

3. I went on vacation _____ my own.

4. I got a check _____ $500 in the mail.

5. There has been a rise _____ the number of violent crimes.

6. The difference _____ you and me is that I don't mind hard work.

7. I can think of no reason _____ her strange behavior.

8. It took a long time to find a solution _____ the problem.

9. I need some information _____ global warming.

10. I'm having trouble _____ my car. It won't start in the morning.

11. In the accident there was quite a lot of damage _____ my car.

12. Investigators are trying to find the cause _____ the accident.

13. I have to do my homework _____ tomorrow.

14. I don't see Craig anymore. I haven't been _____ touch with him for years.

15. Did you get an invitation _____ David's wedding?

*Mr. & Mrs. John Evans*
*Request the honor of your presence*
*at the marriage of their daughter Rose Eleri*
*to David Alastair Austin*
*son of Mr. & Mrs. James Austin*

*at 2:30 P.M. on July 16th, 2011 at*
*St George's Church, Newton, MA*

*~ R.S.V.P. ~*

# Listen

## 8 The vacation of a lifetime

**1** **CD 43** Listen to Neil and Eva's conversation and mark the sentences true (✓) or false (✗).

1. ☐ Neil wants an adventure vacation.
2. ☐ Eva wants an adventure vacation.
3. ☐ They look at some brochures for some ideas.
4. ☐ Eva wants to go to the Maldives to take sailing lessons.
5. ☐ Neil thinks it'll be expensive.
6. ☐ They decide that it might suit them both.

**1** **CD 43** Listen again and complete these lines with the correct linking and commenting expressions.

1. _____, windsurfing is exciting …

2. _____ , I prefer something a bit more relaxing …

3. _____ , we don't get many vacation days a year.

4. _____ , we can find something that suits us both.

5. _____ , you weren't paying attention to a thing I was saying.

6. _____ , there'll be sailing lessons, too.

7. _____ , you can bet your life that it'll cost a fortune.

8. _____ , it's not too bad if you go off-season.

# Pronunciation

## 9 Nouns and verbs

**CD 44** In the chart below the nouns end in an unvoiced sound (/s/, /f/, /θ/) and the verbs end in a voiced sound (/z/, /v/, /ð/). Complete the chart with the words and their final sounds.

| Noun | | Verb | |
|---|---|---|---|
| advice | /s/ | to advise | /z/ |
| | | to use | |
| abuse | | | |
| | /f/ | to believe | |
| relief | | | |
| grief | | | /v/ |
| | | to excuse | |
| breath | | | /ð/ |
| | | to halve | |
| house | | | |
| safe | | | |
| bath | /θ/ | | |

## 10 Emphasis in speaking

**CD 45** Underline the word where the main stress is in **B**'s replies. Then listen and check.

1. **A** Why didn't you do your homework?
   **B** I <u>did</u> do it.

2. **A** Who made this mark on the carpet?
   **B** I did it. Sorry.

3. **A** Did you know that Carlo and Marisa are coming tonight?
   **B** I knew Carlo was coming.

4. **A** Did you know that Carlo and Marisa are coming tonight?
   **B** I knew that ages ago.

5. **A** Who told Mom that I crashed her car?
   **B** I didn't tell her.

6. **A** I wish you hadn't told Mom I crashed her car.
   **B** I didn't tell her.

7. **A** I lost all my money playing cards.
   **B** I told you.

8. **A** You don't like Mike and Annie, do you?
   **B** I like Annie.

9. **A** Why don't you like Annie?
   **B** I do like Annie. I think she's great.

10. **A** I feel so sorry for Annie. Nobody likes her.
    **B** I like her.

# Audio Scripts

## UNIT 1

CD 4

**M = Maggie    J = Jenny**

**M** Jenny! Hi!

**J** Hi, Maggie. I was just passing through, and I thought I'd drop by. Hope that's OK.

**M** Of course, no problem. Come on in. I haven't seen you in a while, Jenny!

**J** I know. Oh, Maggie, you look great. Love the shirt. Love what you're doing with your hair. And you look tan, too.

**M** Thanks, Jenny! I'm just back from vacation, actually. What about you? Tell me what's new!

**J** Nothing much. Work, work, work, 24/7, that's all.

**M** That's too bad. How come you're so busy?

**J** I have a new boss, and she's a little scary. Actually, I'm a little worried I'm going to lose my job.

**M** No. But you've always been so good at your job.

**J** That may be, but she really doesn't like me for some reason. Don't know why.

**M** What are you going to do? Change jobs?

**J** Oh, I hope not. I'm just not up for writing endless letters and going to interviews.

**M** Yeah, job searching stinks. You need a vacation!

**J** Can't afford it. Sam and I are saving up for a new car.

**M** That's ridiculous. Vacations are important.

**J** I know, but Sam's really sick of driving our old car. But maybe you're right. A few days on the beach would help me sort things out a little. OK, I'll talk things over with Sam again and see if I can persuade him.

**M** Good for you.

**J** Thanks, Maggie. You're a good friend.

## UNIT 2

CD 8

**A = Amy    S = Sarah**

**A** Hey, Sarah. What a surprise! How was your weekend in Paris? Did you and Tim love it?

**S** Well, actually, Amy, it was a bit of a disaster. Can you believe he turned up with like three huge suitcases and a hairdryer and stuff like that?

**A** Your husband did? How awful!

**S** Yes, and you should have seen his face when he saw the hotel. You know, it was his first time in Europe. So he kept saying, "The room is so small! The elevator's so small! The staff doesn't speak English!" He probably expected a big American hotel full of Americans.

**A** What a shame!

**S** That's what he thought. Anyway, it went from bad to worse. He hated the food, of course. The first night we had this amazing French meal – French onion soup, roast chicken, beef stew …

**A** Mmm!

**S** I know. But Tim just said, "Yuck. I want a cheeseburger." And when he saw the bill, he just about died. After that he wouldn't spend any money on anything. We had to walk, like, *everywhere*. Even in the park when it started raining.

**A** How ridiculous!

**S** Yeah. I sort of fell down and got mud all over my clothes and everything. What a mess.

**A** Poor you.

**S** Yeah, and by that point I was so upset that I sort of started crying a little. But then Tim felt kind of bad, though, and he apologized and stuff like that.

**A** That's good. How was the rest of the trip?

**S** Really good, actually. Tim calmed down a lot, and on our last day we had a really nice time visiting the museums. We were *both* having fun!

**A** That's great.

**S** I know. Phew! What a relief. And on the flight back we were actually talking about all the terrible things that had happened and just laughing and stuff. Now Tim wants to go back there for our next wedding anniversary.

**A** Wow!

## UNIT 3

CD 12

**B = Becky    M = Mark**

**B** Hey, Mark!

**M** Hi, Becky.

**B** Did you see that show last night on the Reality Channel?

**M** No, I didn't.

**B** It was this amazing story about a family that was separated and then reunited.

**M** Go on. Tell me.

**B** Well, it started like 40 years ago or so, in the '60s. This woman got pregnant, but her husband was a soldier. And right after it happened her husband was sent to fight in Vietnam, and then he went missing over there. So she didn't know what to do. You know, she was pretty young and really poor, so she gave the baby–a baby boy–she gave him up for adoption.

**M** Oh, what a difficult decision. So what happened to the baby's father, then?

**B** Actually, it turned out he was still alive. And when he came home from the war they had another baby, a daughter. But they couldn't find out who had adopted their son because, you know, that information was kept secret back then.

**M** What a shame! That's awful.

**B** And the daughter grew up not knowing she had a brother somewhere. Anyway, the parents kept looking for like 20 years before they finally gave up.

**M** Really? Then what happened?

**B** Apparently, the mother sort of accidentally told her daughter that she had a brother. And so she started to search for him. Well, by that time the daughter had moved to San Francisco, and she'd made some new friends. And one night she went to a dinner party at one of her friends' house. And she was introduced to some new people.

**M** Don't tell me that …

**B** Wait a minute … I haven't finished yet! She got to talking to some guy, and she was telling him how sad she was that she couldn't find her adopted brother. And he was saying, yeah, he understood, 'cause like he was adopted, and he couldn't find his birth mother. And she said she was particularly sad because her brother's birthday was coming up soon on August 9th, and he said that *his* …

**M** I don't believe it!

**B** Yes, that was his birthday, too!

**M** You're kidding! So he was her brother!

**B** Yeah, they had a DNA test to prove it!

**M** I bet the mother was thrilled.

**B** Of course. She couldn't stop crying! And she couldn't believe the number of coincidences that had brought them together. First, they both moved to San Francisco. And they both chose the same area to live in, and then they both made the same friends!

**M** That's amazing! What are the chances of that happening?

# UNIT 4

**CD 14**

I = Interviewer    AP = Adam Phillips

**I** Good evening, I'm Linda Carole, and this is "Looking Back." On today's program, we'll talk about the death of movie star Marilyn Monroe in 1962. It's been over 40 years since she died, but theories concerning her death still fascinate the world. I'm here with Adam Phillips, who is the author of a new book on Marilyn. Adam, welcome to "Looking Back."

**AP** Thank you, Linda.

**I** Now, a lot of our listeners weren't actually around in 1962.

**AP** Right. I don't think you and I were either.

**I** That's right. So let's begin with some background. Do you think you could start by telling us why Marilyn was so famous?

**AP** Sure. I mean, obviously, Marilyn Monroe was beautiful and charming. Her movies were huge hits, very popular. And her life seemed very glamorous–she crossed paths with some of the biggest names of the day.

**I** I wonder if you could give a few examples of that.

**AP** Right. Well, she dated Frank Sinatra, the singer and actor. And of course she knew the president at the time, John F. Kennedy, and also JFK's brother Bobby, who was also a powerful person in the government.

**I** Right.

**AP** But, having said that, I think there's something else people responded to. Marilyn Monroe was, clearly, a very sad person, a very troubled person, and I think people sympathized with that.

**I** Now, in your book, you mention several so-called "conspiracy theories" about her death. Would you mind telling us about some of those theories?

**AP** I'd love to. But first, would you like me to give a little background about her death?

**I** Oh yes, of course, absolutely.

**AP** OK. Marilyn was found dead in bed at her home–this was in Los Angeles–in the early hours of August 5–August 5, 1962–that was a Sunday, I believe. And the police assumed it was a suicide since there was an empty bottle of sleeping pills on the table beside her.

**I** But that's not the whole story, I imagine, is it?

**AP** Oh no, not at all. Several witnesses, including her psychiatrist, insisted she was not suicidal at the time. And other witnesses said they saw Bobby Kennedy visit her house that night, even though he claimed to be in San Francisco.

**I** I see. Very intriguing.

**AP** Yes. And there were other suspicious events–Marilyn's housekeeper, for example. She disappeared immediately after Marilyn's death and wasn't seen for a year. And, Linda, do you happen to know where she turned up a year later?

**I** No, tell me.

**AP** She reappeared as an employee of the Kennedys.

**I** Hmm.

**AP** And because of this, some people have asked–and now, I'm not sure I agree with this, but some have asked, "Why would the Kennedys employ this housekeeper unless they wanted her to keep silent?"

**I** You say "some people" have asked that. Who exactly has suggested the Kennedys might be involved in her death?

**AP** Well, one person was Marilyn's ex-husband, Joe DiMaggio. Joe DiMaggio, of course, was the famous baseball player for the New York Yankees, now dead. DiMaggio was convinced the Kennedys had her killed. He never spoke about it while he was alive, but he wrote about it in his memoirs, which were published as soon as he died.

**I** Very interesting.

**AP** There's also the question of Marilyn's personal diaries, which also disappeared after her death. Now, these diaries–

**I** Oh, I'm really sorry, but I'm afraid we need to take a short break. We'll continue our conversation after these short messages. I'm Linda Carole, and you're listening to "Looking Back."

# UNIT 5

**CD 19**

**Andy and Barry**
A = Andy    B = Barry

**A** So, Barry. It was good to talk to you. Thanks so much for calling.

**B** My pleasure, Andy. By the way, how's your golf game these days? Still playing?

**A** No, not much. I just don't seem to find the time these days. Anyway, Barry ...

**B** What a shame! You used to enjoy it so much.

**A** It's true. OK, Barry. I've got to run. I'm late for a meeting.

**B** OK. Don't want to keep you. So, you'll send me that report?

**A** I'm e-mailing it to you right now. All right. Bye-bye. Have a good weekend!

**B** Same to you! Bye now.

**Richard and Tiffany**
R = Richard    T = Tiffany
C = Computer Operator

**C** Hello, and thank you for calling to activate your new MegaBank credit card. If you are calling from your home phone, please say, "Home phone."

**R** Home phone.

**C** I'm sorry. I didn't understand. If you are calling from your–

**R** Home phone! Home phone!

**C** Thank you. Please enter the sixteen-digit account number of the MegaBank credit card you are calling to activate.

**C** Thank you. Please hold while I transfer you to a customer service representative.

**T** Thank you for calling MegaBank, my name is Tiffany, may I please have your sixteen-digit account number?

**R** But I just entered it a minute ago.

**T** I do apologize for the inconvenience, sir, but I do need to ask you for the account number again.

**R** All right. It's 4-3-5-6, 7-8-1-0, 2-0-2-8, 1-6-0-0.

**T** Thank you. And may I please have your name please, sir?

**R** Richard Clark.

**T** Thank you, Mr. Clark. One moment, please ... Yes, thank you for your patience, Mr. Clark, your card is being activated now.

**R** Good. Thank you.

**T** You're welcome, Mr. Clark. Now, I notice, Mr. Clark, that your account is not enrolled in our Identity Theft Protection Plan. For a small monthly fee–

**R** Sorry, but I'm not interested. And I'm in a bit of a hurry today.

**T** No problem, sir. I'll complete the activation of your card now. Let me just remind you that we are offering a very low interest rate now on balance transfers. Would you like to transfer any balances today?

**R** No, thanks. I really have to go.

**T** Of course, Mr. Clark, and we do thank you for your patience. May I just ask, Mr. Clark, have you considered enrolling in our Credit Assurance Plan? This would protect you in case you lose your job or become sick for a monthly fee of ...

**R** I'm really sorry, Tiffany, but I'm very short on time. Can you just finish activating the card so I can go?

**T** Yes, no problem. Your card is now activated and ready to use. Is there anything else I can help you with today, Mr. Clark?

**R** I don't think so, thanks.

**T** Have a wonderful day, and thank you for choosing MegaBank. Bye now.

**Mario and Amy**
M = Mario    A = Amy

**M** Hello?

**A** Oh, hi, is this Eric?

**M** This is Eric's roommate. Eric's out. Can I take a message?

**A** Oh, Mario. Hi! It's Amy, Eric's friend from math class. We met at Eric's birthday party last month, remember?

**M** Oh, right. Now I remember. Hi, Amy. Well, uh, I'll tell Eric you called. It was good talking to you.

**A**   Oh, wait, Mario. Can you take down a message for me?

**M**   OK. Let me just find a pen here ... OK, I'm ready.

**A**   Can you tell him that our math study group is meeting in a different location?

**M**   Math study group ... different location. Got it. OK, Amy, I'm actually on another call, so ...

**A**   OK, just one second. Can you also tell him that the new location is that coffee shop on Washington Street? It's ...

**M**   No problem, got it. I'll let you go now.

**A**   Wait, it's the coffee shop across from the library, not the one next to the theater.

**M**   Right. Talk to you soon!

**A**   And one more thing. We're meeting at nine, not at eight.

**M**   I'll tell him. Bye, Amy!

**A**   OK, see you!

## UNIT 6

### CD 22

**R = Receptionist    E = Ellen**
**J = James**

**R**   Good morning, LVH Computers. How can I help you?

**E**   Yes, could you put me through to James Barker, please?

**R**   Certainly ... I'm sorry, the line's busy. Do you mind holding?

**E**   OK, that's fine.

**R**   Putting you through now.

**J**   Hello, James Barker.

**E**   James? It's Ellen Miles, from Danson Associates.

**J**   Ellen! How's business?

**E**   Great! Sales are up. But I have a problem with an order I placed with you.

**J**   Oh, I'm sorry. How can I help?

**E**   You know the shipment of laptops we discussed awhile back?

**J**   Oh, yes.

**E**   Well, the order hasn't turned up yet, and you did say that delivery would take a week maximum.

**J**   Well, yes. It usually does. Let me look up the warehouse schedules. Can you bear with me?

**E**   Of course.

**J**   Do you have the order code on hand?

**E**   Yes. Are you ready? It's FED 20457–

**J**   Sorry, you're breaking up. Can you repeat the last part?

**E**   80498.

**J**   Thanks. I'll read that back to you. FED 20457–80498?

**E**   That's right.

**J**   And can you confirm the date of the order for me, please?

**E**   It's August 22nd.

**J**   Well, everything seems to be in order. According to this, the shipment was sent out on September first.

**E**   Well, nothing's arrived.

**J**   I think I'll need to look into it further and get back to you. Are you in the office this afternoon?

**E**   Well, I would be normally, but something's come up. I'm here until 12:00.

**J**   OK. If I don't manage to call you before 12:00, I'll e-mail the information to you.

**E**   Thanks, James. I appreciate your time.

**J**   Don't mention it.

## UNIT 7

### CD 26

**A = Anya    S = Sophie**

**A**   What's wrong, Sophie?

**S**   Oh, nothing much, Anya.

**A**   What do you mean? You look absolutely terrible!

**S**   Oh, I'm just a little bit upset, that's all.

**A**   What about? It's not Ted again, is it?

**S**   Well, yes. He made one or two hurtful remarks this evening.

**A**   One or two? He's always criticizing you these days! I don't know how you can stand it!

**S**   Well, he's been having a little trouble at work recently, so he's pretty stressed.

**A**   Pretty stressed? That's no excuse for being cruel. I think his behavior is totally out of line.

**S**   Yeah, it's getting me down a little.

**A**   Well, you really shouldn't put up with it any longer, Sophie. You should tell him that if he can't be nicer to you, you won't go out with him anymore.

**S**   Oh, I suppose so. But the trouble is, I'm really crazy about him, you know.

**A**   Well, that's obvious, or you wouldn't put up with all his terrible behavior.

**S**   And he loves me, too. I know it.

**A**   Well, he's got a funny way of showing it.

**S**   I suppose you're right. Our relationship hasn't been great lately. We haven't been getting along very well.

**A**   No kidding. You've both been completely miserable. Honestly, Sophie, you must do something about it. It's no good waiting until things get magically better. It isn't going to happen.

**S**   OK, OK, Anya. I'll talk to him tonight, I promise.

### CD 27

| | |
|---|---|
| 1. doesn't | 6. arranged |
| 2. shouldn't | 7. relationship |
| 3. promised | 8. comfortable |
| 4. strapped | 9. excitement |
| 5. special | 10. impressed |

## UNIT 8

### CD 30

**Alex**

Yeah, I'm from Chicago, so I'm used to a lot of extreme weather. It's hot, hot, hot in the summer and freezing cold in the winter. And it's windy, obviously, which is why they call it the "Windy City." And it rains all the time. But I'd say my worst experience with extreme weather wasn't in Chicago, actually. It was out in the woods. I went camping with my wife, Judy, which was a bad idea because I just knew she'd hate it. She's a city girl who loves museums and movies and restaurants. And we'd just gotten married, so we still didn't know each other that well ... *and* the weather report said there was a good chance of rain, which was a recipe for disaster when you put it all together. I guess I just wanted to show her that I was a really tough, cool, outdoorsy guy.

But, anyway, we put up the tent, which went fine. So far, so good. But in the middle of the night the bad weather set in. The wind was really blowing the tent around, and then my Judy started crying, saying she was scared, which was understandable since the tent was about to fly away! And I was trying to reassure her and saying it wasn't so bad when all of the sudden, the wind really started blowing the tent over. And then I dropped my flashlight and it went all dark, which was bad because Judy's kind of afraid of the dark. And she just freaked out and started running through the woods with her sleeping bag over her head. And, well, I ran after her and fell over into a pool of this disgusting muddy stuff. It was all over me, which was too bad since I didn't have another change of clothes with me. In the end I had to throw those clothes away. Anyway, after that we just stuffed the gear in the car and drove home. I really felt stupid about the whole episode. And the car smelled really awful the whole way back, which was like two hours or so. Now we think about it and just laugh, but it was awful at the time.

**Sam**

Well, one time that sticks out in my mind was back when I was in college, and I was doing this summer internship, which is where you go work at a company for free just to get the experience. And they always tell you that you're going to do all these exciting things, but then, in reality, they just have you make photocopies all summer long, which is obviously really disappointing. So I was doing my internship at this bank downtown and living at my cousin's apartment, which was too far from downtown to walk. And since I wasn't being paid, I had to save money by riding my bike to work, which was really awful because I also had to wear a suit and tie. So I'd always be really worried that I'd get bicycle grease on my suit or get splashed by a puddle or something. Anyway, to make a long story short, I really hated that internship. And not only that, I hated the whole thing—wearing a fancy suit, being in an office, thinking about money all the time—which was a great thing to realize. That's why I decided to change my major and become a teacher.

But, anyway, the last day of my internship was in August, I think, which can be a very rainy month in Chicago. And as I was riding my bike away from that office building, the sky just opened up. I mean, my clothes really got soaking wet, which normally would have been very upsetting. But since my internship was over now, I wasn't worried about ruining my fancy suit. I just didn't care. It felt great! And I just remember pedaling down the street happy as can be, laughing and laughing—and maybe singing, even!—in a three-piece suit that was just totally soaking wet. Everyone was staring at me like I was crazy!

# UNIT 9

**CD** **33**

**K = Kathy**    **E = Eric**

**K**  Oh, Eric, look at this article, more terrible news about global warming. An iceberg was spotted floating near New Zealand. Imagine that. All the way up there!

**E**  I suppose that could mean it's getting colder. Am I right, Kathy? Maybe it's a good thing.

**K**  Don't be silly. It says this is happening because there used to be all this ice in Antarctica, around the South Pole, but it's all melting now. And these big chunks of ice are breaking off and floating away. You know, if you ask me, it's time we did something about global warming.

**E**  You mean, like, you and me? What can we do?

**K**  No, not just you and me. Everyone. My point is, we're running out of time. As far as I understand it, all the ice is going to melt soon. And once it does, all sorts of horrible things will happen. Flooding, famine, disease …

**E**  Maybe we should buy property a few miles from the ocean. That way, when the sea levels rise we'll have a beautiful beachfront house!

**K**  Be serious! What really worries me is that our children will have to deal with these problems.

**E**  I know, but to tell you the truth, I'm not sure there's anything we can do. As far as I'm concerned, I'm not even sure that global warming is real.

**K**  Oh, you must be kidding.

**E**  No. I mean, wasn't it unusually cool this summer? And the summer before that? Remember how hot it used to be in the kitchen in August?

**K**  Oh, come on, be serious.

**E**  I *am* being serious. As I was saying, how can the world be getting warmer when the weather here is so cool?

**K**  That's not the point. Global warming is about patterns in the weather over many, many years in lots of different places, not just what happened last summer.

**E**  OK, I know you're right. The planet *is* warmer than it used to be. But another thing is that we don't know why this is happening. Maybe it's caused by pollution but maybe not.

**K**  Well, I'm no scientist, but I'm pretty sure pollution causes it. Anyway, the point I'm trying to make is that we can't just sit around doing nothing. I mean, even if it turns out pollution doesn't cause global warming, it still wouldn't hurt to reduce it. Right?

**E**  Hmm, that is true. The smog around here can get pretty awful sometimes. When I was a kid the air used to be a lot cleaner. But still, what can we do about it?

**K**  Well, for one thing, we could drive less often and take more walks. Remember when we were first married, how we would just go for walks in the park and watch the sun set?

**E**  Yeah, that was nice. How about we go for a walk now?

**K**  Oh, I'd love that. I'll just get my coat.

# UNIT 10

**CD** **37**

**A = Alicia**    **B = Beth**

**A**  So, Beth, how's your little sister getting along with your parents these days?

**B**  Thanks for asking, Alicia. They're getting a long a lot better. They had a big heart-to-heart talk last weekend, and that helped.

**A**  So what was the problem, then?

**B**  Well, for one thing, since I moved into my own apartment I've had my hands full with setting everything up, so I haven't been to my parents' home very often. My sister's having to face the fact that she's the only child left at home now. And that's hard for everyone.

**A**  You can say that again.

**B**  Also, my parents wanted her to go to college. She tried, but her heart wasn't in it. She wants to open her own store.

**A**  Yes, she has a very good head for business, doesn't she?

**B**  Yes, she's always been good with money. Anyway, she told my parents that they had to stop trying to run her life for her.

**A**  Ouch. She probably shouldn't have said that. But she's always had a bit of a sharp tongue, hasn't she?

**B**  Yes, but she didn't really mean it. She was just upset.

**A**  Oh, I know. But how did your parents react?

**B**  They were really hurt. Anyway, she apologized. And now–guess what? They're all going into business together!

**A**  Wow, you must be pulling my leg! I wouldn't have predicted that!

**B**  I know. I couldn't believe it when they told me.

**A**  So they're starting a store, then?

**B**  Yes. The store opens in three months, and my parents are going to give her a hand with running it.

**A**  That's great!

# UNIT 11

**CD** **41**

**G = Greg**    **M = Mark**

**G**  Hello, Mark. I just came to see how you were doing with setting up your home office. How's it going?

**M**  Greg! Come in, come in. Well, I've spent all morning on it, but I haven't made much progress, if any.

**G**  How come?

**M**  Well, I can't get my new computer to work, for one thing, and I can't even set up my new computer table. It's turning into a nightmare already.

**G**  What a pain! Need any help?

**M**  If you've got a minute, that'd be great! Look at this. These instructions don't make any sense at all. How do the legs fit onto there?

**G**  Oh, don't ask me! You should have seen me trying to put together my new dresser. What a joke! You'd have had a good laugh if you'd been there. Anyway, let me take a look.

**M**  Here you are.

**G**  Hmm. I think there are some parts missing. Look at the diagram here. You need a small thing like that to put these together.

**M**  Oh, I can't believe it! You mean they didn't give me all the parts? You've got to be kidding. I'm going to call and complain right now. Oh, I wish I'd never bought the stupid thing in the first place. I should have remembered that I'm no good at this sort of thing.

**G**  Calm down, Mark. If worse comes to worst, they'll just have to give you your money back.

**M** It's just that I'm sick of the whole thing already. And I've still got to try to fix the computer.

**G** I know, I know. This sort of thing drives me crazy, too. Oh, look, what's this at the bottom of the box? Here are your missing parts, if I'm not mistaken!

**M** Oh, what an idiot I am. I could kick myself. Thanks, Greg. You saved the day. Let me take you out for coffee tomorrow.

**G** Well, if all goes well from now on, you might just be finished by then!

# UNIT 12

**CD 43**

N = Neil      E = Eva

**N** I want to do something different for our vacation this year, ideally something adventurous for a change.

**E** Really? What kind of thing?

**N** Don't know, actually. Maybe going to a lake and learning water sports? Apparently, windsurfing is exciting, and we could also learn to sail.

**E** It doesn't sound like much fun to me. Personally, I prefer something a bit more relaxing. I think we work hard enough all year so that we deserve to do nothing somewhere nice for a couple of weeks.

**N** But I'm sick of lying on a beach and stuff like that. We can do that any old time. It's time we had some new experiences in life. After all, we don't get many vacation days a year.

**E** Well, obviously, I'm very impressed with your new lease on life. However, I'm still not sure what you have in mind or if I want to do it, too.

**N** Let's look on the Internet and see what kinds of things there are. Hopefully, we can find something that suits us both.

**E** Oh, OK then, but I'm not promising anything.

**E** Oh, look. Now that's what I call a vacation!

**N** The Maldives? Small beach islands in the middle of the Indian Ocean? Not on your life! Obviously, you weren't paying attention to a thing I was saying. Anyway, they're way too expensive.

**E** No, but look! Look what you can do! There are windsurfing and scuba-diving lessons. Presumably, there'll be sailing lessons, too. Yes, look. Sailing. Even something called "parasailing." No idea what that is, though.

**N** Hmm. Sounds interesting, actually. Still, you can bet your life that it'll cost a fortune.

**E** In fact, it's not too bad if you go off-season. Look here at the prices. And off-season a lot of activities are included in the price. Oh, please, let's go. Personally, I've always wanted to go to a desert island. It looks so peaceful. It'll be the vacation of a lifetime!

**N** But you don't want an adventure vacation.

**E** I don't have to have one. I can lie on the beach and watch you exhausting yourself. That's my idea of a good time!

# Phonetic symbols

| | Consonants | | | |
|---|---|---|---|---|
| 1 | /p/ | as in | **pen** | /pɛn/ |
| 2 | /b/ | as in | **big** | /bɪg/ |
| 3 | /t/ | as in | **tea** | /ti/ |
| 4 | /d/ | as in | **do** | /du/ |
| 5 | /k/ | as in | **cat** | /kæt/ |
| 6 | /g/ | as in | **go** | /goʊ/ |
| 7 | /f/ | as in | **five** | /faɪv/ |
| 8 | /v/ | as in | **very** | /ˈvɛri/ |
| 9 | /s/ | as in | **son** | /sʌn/ |
| 10 | /z/ | as in | **zoo** | /zu/ |
| 11 | /l/ | as in | **live** | /lɪv/ |
| 12 | /m/ | as in | **my** | /maɪ/ |
| 13 | /n/ | as in | **nine** | /naɪn/ |
| 14 | /h/ | as in | **happy** | /ˈhæpi/ |
| 15 | /r/ | as in | **red** | /rɛd/ |
| 16 | /y/ | as in | **yes** | /yɛs/ |
| 17 | /w/ | as in | **want** | /wɒnt/ |
| 18 | /θ/ | as in | **thanks** | /θæŋks/ |
| 19 | /ð/ | as in | **the** | /ðə/ |
| 20 | /ʃ/ | as in | **she** | /ʃi/ |
| 21 | /ʒ/ | as in | **television** | /ˈtelɪvɪʒn/ |
| 22 | /tʃ/ | as in | **child** | /tʃaɪld/ |
| 23 | /dʒ/ | as in | **Japan** | /dʒəˈpæn/ |
| 24 | /ŋ/ | as in | **English** | /ˈɪŋglɪʃ/ |

| | Vowels | | | |
|---|---|---|---|---|
| 25 | /i/ | as in | **see** | /si/ |
| 26 | /ɪ/ | as in | **his** | /hɪz/ |
| 27 | /ɛ/ | as in | **ten** | /tɛn/ |
| 28 | /æ/ | as in | **stamp** | /stæmp/ |
| 29 | /ɑ/ | as in | **father** | /ˈfɑðər/ |
| 30 | /ɔ/ | as in | **saw** | /sɔ/ |
| 31 | /ʊ/ | as in | **book** | /bʊk/ |
| 32 | /u/ | as in | **you** | /yu/ |
| 33 | /ʌ/ | as in | **sun** | /sʌn/ |
| 34 | /ə/ | as in | **about** | /əˈbaʊt/ |
| 35 | /eɪ/ | as in | **name** | /neɪm/ |
| 36 | /aɪ/ | as in | **my** | /maɪ/ |
| 37 | /ɔɪ/ | as in | **boy** | /bɔɪ/ |
| 38 | /aʊ/ | as in | **how** | /haʊ/ |
| 39 | /oʊ/ | as in | **go** | /goʊ/ |
| 40 | /ər/ | as in | **bird** | /bərd/ |
| 41 | /ɪr/ | as in | **near** | /nɪr/ |
| 42 | /ɛr/ | as in | **hair** | /hɛr/ |
| 43 | /ar/ | as in | **car** | /kar/ |
| 44 | /ɔr/ | as in | **more** | /mɔr/ |
| 45 | /ʊr/ | as in | **tour** | /tʊr/ |

# SPOTLIGHT ON TESTING

---

**Requirements in reading / listening**

Many reading/listening passages (job descriptions, directions, etc.) mention some required things as well as some optional things. Test questions may ask you to distinguish between what is required and what is optional.

---

**1 Understanding Requirements**

A. Read the job announcements.

## ManagerNet Job Clearinghouse

**I) Job: Quality Control Manager**
**Employer: Seaboard Technologies, Inc.**
**Duties:**

- Oversee quality control testing of computer memory chips and other products
- Manage 20-person technical staff
- Maintain relations with customers and suppliers
- Contribute to company's strategic planning for the future

**Qualifications:**

- Master's degree in management, industrial engineering, or closely related field
- Five years experience in quality control, preferably in management
- Budgeting experience, experience in controlling costs a plus
- Willingness to travel frequently, often overseas
- Excellent communication skills

Contact: Human Resources Manager, Seaboard Technologies, Inc., 57 Port Road, Natick, MA 01760 humres@seaboardnatick.com

**2) Job: Product Development Manager**
**Employer: Hammer Cycle Sports, Inc.**
**Duties:**

- Lead staff in the development of new products and services
- Assess customer satisfaction and respond to customer needs
- Direct training of adventure guides and sales representatives
- Keep up-to-date about improvements in technology and industry standards
- Manage product-development budget

**Qualifications:**

- High school diploma, some college preferred
- Current knowledge of extreme sports, especially cycle sports
- Ability to participate in company-provided adventure travel programs
- Excellent personal communication skills
- Budgeting experience a plus

Contact: Mr. Devon Cole, Hammer Cycle Sports, Inc., 3411 Lincoln Hwy, St. George, UT 84711 coledevon@hammerbikes.net

B. Circle the letter of the best option.

1. The person hired for the Seaboard Technologies job is required to have
   a. a college degree.
   b. five years' experience in management.
   c. experience controlling costs.

2. Which qualification is optional for the Hammer Cycle Sports job?

   a. High school graduation

   b. Knowledge about extreme sports

   c. Budgeting experience

3. _____ is required for both jobs.

   a. Budgeting experience

   b. The ability to communicate well

   c. A college degree

### Making inferences

To fully understand a reading/listening passage, you might have to "read between the lines." Some test questions ask you to **make inferences**—to understand what is not said directly. Use clues from the context, logic, and your own experience.

## 2 Practicing with inferences

Check (✓) each statement that can be strongly inferred from the job announcements.

1. ☐ Seaboard Technologies has customers and/or suppliers in other countries.

2. ☐ Hammer Cycle Sports does not require an intelligent person.

3. ☐ Both jobs require the ability to handle money well.

## 3 Making inferences from personal statements

AUDIO FILE 🔊 Listen to the personal statements. Check (✓) the two strongest inferences from what each person says.

Ted

1. ☐ Seals are dangerous.

2. ☐ La Jolla is on the seacoast.

3. ☐ There are more seals now than in Ted's childhood.

Lucia

4. ☐ The Amazon is bigger than the Tapajos.

5. ☐ The Tapajos is strong enough to carry away a house.

6. ☐ The river east of Santarem is not half brown and half blue.

Mari

7. ☐ There are restaurants near the Kifissia train station.

8. ☐ Mari has relatives living in Kifissia.

9. ☐ The Penteli mountain has fewer forests now than in Mari's childhood.

## 4 Check your understanding

AUDIO FILE 🔊 Listen again to the personal statements. Write T for true or F for false.

1. ____ Ted had to walk from downtown San Diego to La Jolla.

2. ____ Lucia has to stay out of the rivers in Santarem.

3. ____ Mari's family had to take a taxi from Kifissia to Penteli.

4. ____ People in La Jolla have to stay out of the Children's Pool.

> Remember that modal verbs tell you a lot. *Have to* and *must* can show requirements. *Could* or *might* often show optional things.

## 5 Skills in review

Look again at Exercise 5 on p. 4 of the Workbook. In what ways does Thomas reflect both Korean and American cultures?

## Identifying reasons

Test questions may ask about the reason for an action. Words like *because* or *reason* may be clues. Also, remember who is speaking or writing. The identity may be a clue to the reason.

### 1 Understanding reasons

A. Read the e-mail.

| | |
|---|---|
| **To:** | Kyle Peters <petersk@seebolt.com>   CC: Heather Fortin <fortin@seebolt.org> |
| **From:** | Debra Bannas |
| **Date:** | January 15 |
| **Subject:** | Toy Quality |

Hi Kyle,

I just talked to Jim Decker at the San Francisco office. The issue is a shipment of toys now on the docks in S.F.  Apparently, we've got three shipping containers there, but Jim doesn't want to sign for them because there's a problem with the paperwork. The shipper did not send a certification that the toys are lead-free. As you know, Seebolt policy is really strict about that, and Jim doesn't want to take a chance.  We definitely don't want to sell any toys with lead in them. We could land in court, and more importantly, we would never, ever want to sell dangerous toys.

However, NOT signing could have serious costs. We've never had any trouble with this manufacturer— never any lead, always good quality, etc. If we refuse the shipment, we could lose a good supplier. If the shipment is really OK and we let it stay on dock for a long time, we'd have to pay storage fees at $800 per day! Jim has been trying for a whole day to reach the supplier but can't get through to anyone in management. Apparently, he can't even get through to anyone who speaks English. I told Jim I'd bring it up to you. What's your advice? Should he risk it and sign? Thanks in advance for your help.

Debra

B. Check (✓) the reason for each action or situation.

1. Why Jim Decker called:
   ☐ to get advice about what to do   ☐ to complain about the supplier   ☐ to say he accepted the shipment

2. Why the company could land in court:
   ☐ selling toys that contain lead   ☐ getting certification from the supplier   ☐ using another supplier

3. Why signing might be good:
   ☐ making sure the shipment does not get stolen   ☐ helping Jim Decker keep his job
   ☐ not having to pay $800 a day

4. Why Jim could not solve the problem:
   ☐ dangerous materials inside the shipment   ☐ not being able to reach an English speaker
   ☐ the large size of the shipment

Strategies for taking the:   **TOEFL® Test**   **TOEIC® Test**   **IELTS™ Test**

On tests, reading and listening passages often mention difficulties. Questions may ask what is difficult and how the difficulty might be overcome.

## 2 Understanding difficulties

Read the e-mail again. Write *T* for true or *F* for false.

1. ____ Three containers of toys did not arrive on time.

2. ____ The supplier did not send some necessary papers.

3. ____ The supplier has made many similar mistakes in the past.

4. ____ Jim Decker cannot speak English.

## 3 Understanding difficulties in listening

AUDIO FILE 🔊 Listen to the TV program. Circle the letter of the correct answer.

1. Why couldn't gold seekers travel to California by train?
   a. The trains in 1849 could not travel through mountainous areas.
   b. Trains drew more Indian attacks than other forms of transportation.
   c. There was no train service from the East to California until 1868.

2. Which is NOT mentioned in the program as a difficulty faced by gold seekers traveling to California by land?
   a. diseases
   b. snow
   c. Indian attacks

3. What is mentioned in the program as a difficulty faced by many gold seekers traveling to California by sea?
   a. They had to travel through storms at the southern tip of South America.
   b. They had to cross high mountains after reaching San Francisco.
   c. They had to pay high prices for their trip.

4. Why, according to the program, did some 49ers arrive "too sick and weak to go looking for gold?"
   a. They had to work hard on the ships that carried them to California.
   b. They had caught malaria or yellow fever in Panama.
   c. The sea trip to California took eight months.

## 4 Skills in review

Look again at Exercise 8 on p. 14 of the Workbook. Now read the e-mail (above) about Seebolt. Underline the prepositions in the e-mail.

> It's sometimes hard to hear *to* in speech. Some "purpose" clues are verbs like *try*, *want*, and *hope.*

# Unit 3 | Past and simultaneous actions/events

## References to the past

Some reading/listening passages might not be linear (going forward in a straight line). Some start at one point in time but then tell about things in the past. Adverbials (e.g., *earlier, before this, two years ago*) or verb forms (e.g., the past perfect) might indicate this.

### 1 Understanding references to the past

A. Read the character descriptions.

## Main Characters in *The Great Gatsby*

F. Scott Fitzgerald's *The Great Gatsby* (published 1925) takes place mostly in West Egg, a rich community on Long Island. It is set in the 1920s. The main characters are as follows:

**Nick Carraway**—The narrator of the story, Carraway lives in a West Egg house next to the mansion where Jay Gatsby lives. (See notes about Gatsby, below.) He was raised in Minnesota and went to Yale University. Nick's upbringing in the Midwest conferred upon him a quiet, thoughtful personality and a moderate lifestyle. This sets him apart from the novel's other characters and makes him a trustworthy narrator. After Yale, he went to New York City to work as a bond trader. We assume he did well because he can afford to live in West Egg. There he reconnects with his cousin Daisy Buchanan and her husband, Tom Buchanan, whom Nick had socialized with in college. Nick has a short-lived romance with Jordan Baker, a famous female golfer and a friend of Daisy's. Eventually, Nick rejects the "careless" lifestyle of Jordan, Daisy, and Tom and moves back to the Midwest.

**Jay Gatsby**—Fabulously wealthy, Gatsby hosts wild parties every Saturday, which many of the novel's characters—including Nick on occasion—attend. Through much of the novel, mystery surrounds Gatsby's background—not only his personal origins but the source of his wealth. Gatsby and Nick become friends, and Nick learns that Gatsby had once been romantically involved with Nick's cousin, Daisy. Through spending time with Nick, Gatsby and Daisy briefly revive their relationship, despite Daisy's marriage to Tom. Their romance is destroyed after a tragic accident. As Nick eventually finds out, Gatsby was born as James Gatz to a poor family in the midwestern state of North Dakota. He was ambitious and eventually created his new East Coast personality, making his money primarily through bootlegging (illegally selling) alcohol. (The United States had laws against possessing alcohol from 1920 to 1933.) The novel gradually reveals that Gatsby's public image as a confident sophisticate hides an insecure, naïve, and surprisingly gentle man. Gatsby meets an untimely death. A touching scene near the end of the novel involves Gatsby's father, Henry Gatz, who has come to West Egg for the funeral. Gatz finds a book Gatsby had as a child and points proudly to a schedule the boy had written for himself—a sign that Gatsby had been organized and ambitious even as a child.

B. Circle the letter of the best answer.

1. Which did NOT happen before Nick first met Tom Buchanan?
   a. He moved to West Egg.
   b. He started studying at Yale.
   c. He was raised in Minnesota.

Strategies for taking the:   TOEFL® Test      TOEIC® Test      IELTS™ Test

2. The story starts with Nick living in a West Egg house. What came before that?

    a. He met Jay Gatsby.
    b. He did well as a bond trader.
    c. He reconnected with his cousin Daisy.

3. Which of the following happened before Nick met Jay Gatsby?

    a. Gatsby invented an "East Coast personality."
    b. Gatsby revived a romance with Daisy.
    c. Gatsby's father found a book in Gatsby's house.

### Time in narratives: events at the same time

A **linear** narrative tells a story directly from beginning to end. On tests, narratives may have non-linear parts. Events might happen **simultaneously**—at the same time. Look for clues like *while, meanwhile, also at this time,* etc.

## 2 Practice with simultaneous events

Read the character descriptions again. Check (✓) the pair of simultaneous events.

1. ☐ Nick moves to West Egg. / Daisy and Gatsby revive their relationship.

2. ☐ Gatsby gets rich through bootlegging. / United States has Prohibition.

3. ☐ Nick attends a Saturday night party at Gatsby's. / Nick rejects the "careless" lifestyle of Daisy's social set.

## 3 Check your understanding

Read the character descriptions again. Write T for true or F for false.

1. ____ Gatsby and Daisy get together again.

2. ____ Neither Gatsby nor Nick was born on the East Coast.

3. ____ Gatsby eventually marries Daisy.

4. ____ Gatsby became rich as a bond trader.

## 4 Understanding simultaneous actions

AUDIO FILE 🔊 Listen to the police officer interviewing three witnesses to a crime. Write the letter of the action that is simultaneous with each action on the left.

1. ____ Witness 1, riding behind the mini-mall,

2. ____ Witness 1, watching the man in a tan coat and baseball cap,

3. ____ Witness 2, noticing a small area of light,

4. ____ Witness 2, seeing a light shine on a jewelry case,

5. ____ Witness 3, getting to the alley,

6. ____ The man, looking straight at Witness 3,

    a. watches a hammer come down on the case.
    b. reaches inside his coat.
    c. realizes that the light came from a flashlight.
    d. sees a man scooping jewels into a gym bag.
    e. sees a parked truck.
    f. dials 911.

## 5 Skills in review

Look again at Exercise 3 on p. 17 of the Workbook. Summarize the information (above) about either Nick Carraway or Jay Gatsby. Use the narrative tenses.

If a test question asks for background or reasons (e.g., *Why did Gatsby create a new personality?*), it is asking for references to the past. Look for the signals.

# Unit 4 | Disbelief and evidence

## Adjectives of disbelief

Some test questions ask not just *whether* a speaker/writer disbelieves
something but also how strong that disbelief is. Some adjectives (e.g., *unlikely*)
show moderate doubt. Others (e.g., *ridiculous*) show stronger doubt. You have to
understand the difference.

### 1 Understanding expressions of disbelief

A. Read the article.

## Crop Circles: Not Much of a Mystery

When strange patterns suddenly appear in fields of grain, people go a little crazy. Typically, a farmer discovers that one of these "crop circles" has appeared in his field overnight. One evening, all the crops are standing. The next morning, some of his corn or wheat has been pressed down into a perfect circle or even into an elaborate set of swoops and swirls.

The most popular explanation is that alien spacecraft make crop circles. [A. Supposedly, an alien ship comes down from outer space and either lands or presses crops down with a power burst. This is a silly conclusion, but farmers back in 1978, when the first modern crop circles appeared, could be forgiven for jumping to it. How could anything else make such big circles so fast?] And the design of the circle becomes clear only from above. [B. Farmers today, and the gullible public, should be embarrassed for even considering that flaky explanation. Two British men, Doug Bower and Dave Chorley, admitted that they made the 1978 circles as a joke. Since then, countless jokers have created crop circles and then bragged

about it.] There have even been competitions for crop-circle art. Clearly, any theory that says humans could not have made the circles is totally bogus.

[C. A little less goofy are some other non-human origins for the circles—certain weather events. Some people have suggested that a phenomenon called "ball lightning" could make the circles.] As its name suggests, it is reported to be spherical and therefore consistent with circular marks. [D. The problem is that no reliable evidence shows that ball lightning even exists, and serious scientists consider all reports of it doubtful.] Other people have suggested that small, intense, and very local vortexes of wind descend on fields and create circles. Again, however, no reliable witness has ever observed any such winds at crop-circle locations.

The bottom line is that a lot of evidence links tricksters or even oddball artists to crop circles, and no solid evidence supports any other explanation.

B. Look at the four bracketed sentences [A–D] in Part A. Write the number from the line below that best describes the author's attitude toward each bracketed idea. (Different students may come up with different answers.)

Some Doubt    1      2      3      4    Strong Doubt

A. ____

B. ____

C. ____

D. ____

Strategies for taking the:   **TOEFL® Test**   **TOEIC® Test**   **IELTS™ Test**

**Evidence** is a detail that most readers or listeners accept as true. It is used to support an idea—to make the idea stronger or more believable. As you read or listen, understand how evidence and ideas connect to each other.

## 2 Recognizing evidence

Read the article again. Check (✓) each statement that is a piece of evidence—each fact.

1. ☐ Circles or other designs appear in fields of crops.
2. ☐ An alien ship from outer space lands in the field.
3. ☐ Bower and Chorley admit to creating a hoax.
4. ☐ Ball lighting creates a circle in a field.

## 3 Connecting evidence and ideas

AUDIO FILE 🔊 Listen to the conversation. Circle the letter of the best answer.

1. What evidence for a ghost did the security cameras show?

   a. the laundry room of a dorm
   b. a white shape in the corner
   c. an article in the newspaper

2. What evidence indicated that students sensed a ghost?

   a. Students screamed and ran from the room.
   b. Students stopped using the laundry room.
   c. Students suddenly acted cold or looked around.

3. What evidence for a ghost has been observed outside the laundry room?

   a. A white sheet has floated through the dorm.
   b. An elevator moves for no real reason.
   c. A spooky voice has been recorded.

## 4 Check your understanding

AUDIO FILE 🔊 Listen to the conversation again. Write T for true or F for false.

1. ____ Ford Hall is a dormitory.

2. ____ The recording of the ghost was made by students.

3. ____ Fred knows that no one really died at Ford Hall.

2. ____ Tina thinks there is good evidence showing that a ghost is in the dorm.

## 5 Skills in review

Look again at Exercise 5 on p. 24 of the Workbook. What evidence convinced people to accept Frank Abagnale as a pilot and a lawyer?

> Do you hear an expression of doubt in a test conversation? Listen for a reason for that doubt. People who write tests usually include reasons.

# Unit 5 | Problems and solutions

### Understanding problems

A test question might ask you to identify one or more problems in a reading or listening passage. Expressions like *trouble*, *unfortunately*, and *problem* might indicate one. Also, statements with *but* or *however* might introduce a problem.

**1  Practice recognizing problems and solutions**

A. Read the magazine article.

## What to Do with the *Titanic* Treasure?

The sinking of the ship *Titanic* in 1912 remains one of the most famous disasters of modern times. Going down with the ship were 1,522 people. Some of them undoubtedly left valuable jewelry on the ship, but *Titanic* carried no large quantity of gold or money. Nevertheless, every item in or on the wreck, even a plain piece of iron from the hull, has huge historical value. One of the biggest questions surrounding the *Titanic* now is, "Who owns the immense treasure?"

For decades, no one knew where the wreck was. The ship's surface location when it sank was documented, but its resting place on the bottom was hard to determine. The problem was that the *Titanic* went down where ocean waters are 2.5 miles deep. Then, in 1985, the well-known American oceanographer Robert Ballard demonstrated that the *Titanic* lay on the ocean floor 963 miles northeast of New York City. This spot is in international waters. Ballard has argued that the wreck should be a protected international monument and that disturbing it should be illegal. He, of course, has never claimed to own it.

Most sunken ships are legally the property of the company that owned the ship while it sailed. However, this principle doesn't work for the *Titanic*. Because it was considered impossible to raise, the ship was not mentioned in sale documents when its owner, the White Star Line, was sold to Cunard Lines. Cunard's claims to the ship have not been supported in court. An almost incredible number of insurance companies— more than 700—banded together in the early 1990s to claim that, since they paid out money for losses in the disaster, they owned the wreck. Their claims were settled privately out of court, for undisclosed amounts of money, in 1994.

That same year, a court in Virginia gave a company named RMS Titanic, Inc. (RMST) "salvage rights." This, however, does not solve the ownership problem. RMST may remove items from the ship and may put them on display in public shows, but the company does not own them. Since then, RMST has been pleading for at least partial ownership of the precious artifacts. They point out that their many expeditions to recover items are too costly to be covered by admission fees from exhibits. They face big obstacles. Some courts in the U.S. and the U.K. have ruled that no one can ever own the wreck because it is, as Ballard argues, an international treasure. Ballard wants the courts, additionally, to declare that no one may even touch the wreck. Tourists have been descending in tough submersible ships and landing on the *Titanic*. Seawater eats away at the ship, which Ballard says is now so weak that the pressure of any landing could make it collapse.

B. Circle the letter of the best answer.

1. Why was it hard to locate the wreck of the *Titanic*?

   a. No one knew where it was when it sank.

   b. It sank in very deep water.

   c. It fell apart as it sank.

2. Why was the *Titanic* not sold to Cunard along with other property of the White Star Line?

   a. The companies believed the wreck could not be recovered.

   b. There was nothing valuable in the wreck.

   c. A sunken ship is not owned by the company that operated it.

Strategies for taking the:   TOEFL® Test    TOEIC® Test    IELTS™ Test

3. Even though they were given salvage rights to the *Titanic*, RMST is unhappy. What problem do they have?

    a. Tourists have been damaging the wreck of the ship.

    b. They haven't yet found anything valuable on the wreck.

    c. They can't make enough money by showing the *Titanic* artifacts.

## 2 Check your understanding

Read the magazine article again. Write T for true or F for false.

1. ____ More than 1,500 people died in the sinking of the *Titanic*.

2. ____ The seafloor where the *Titanic* rests is inside the United States.

3. ____ Robert Ballard claims to own the *Titanic*.

4. ____ The structure of the wreck gets weaker year by year.

**Choosing the best solution**

Reading and listening passages about problems usually mention solutions.
Several solutions may be mentioned where you have to choose the best one.
Listen (or read) for positive word clues like *the best*, *practical*, or *probably*.

## 3 Understanding a conversation about problems and solutions

AUDIO FILE 🔊 Listen to the conversation. Circle the word or phrase that best completes each statement.

1. Jen's problem with the wedding is caused by (scheduled exams / lack of money / her sister's poor health).

2. Three of Jen's professors have said they will not be (strict / concerned / flexible) about exam dates.

3. Jen doesn't want to (go to the wedding / talk to her professors / take her exams) because she would be embarrassed.

4. Brad suggests that Jen could take a (grade / class / exam) of incomplete.

5. Jen is afraid she might (be embarrassed / fail her classes / lose her scholarship) if she had three incompletes.

6. Brad suggests that Jen's (professors / advisor / parents) could write letters asking for flexibility in the exam schedule.

## 4 One-Minute Speaking Task

AUDIO FILE 🔊 Some tests (like the TOEFL®) use a problem-related conversation as part of a speaking task. Listen again to the conversation between Jen and Brad. They discuss three possible solutions to Jen's problem. In 60 seconds (use a timer), describe her problem and the three solutions. Then say what the best solution is and why you think so. (Try recording and listening to your own response, or try the speaking task with your teacher.)

## 5 Skills in review

What do you think will happen to the wreck of the *Titanic*? Look again at Exercises 2 and 4 on pp. 29–30 of the Workbook. Use these future verb forms in your answer.

> To answer questions about possible solutions, listen for good and bad points. The solution with few or no bad points is probably the answer.

**SPOTLIGHT ON TESTING**

Test questions about organization may ask what group an idea fits into. The question may name categories and ask you to put ideas into them. As you read or listen, sort these ideas in your mind.

### 1 Practice with categories

A. Read the advertisement.

# Get the Best Apps with Bandwidth!

Like your handheld? You'll love it with a Sweet Suite of apps from Bandwidth Synergies. We are America's top shop for networking, games, music, and everything else for your i-Life. Check out our Sweet Suites, packaging the apps you like best for less than half of what you would pay to buy them singly. (Each Suite $24.99)

### Suite #1 – The Manhattan
Feel the city vibe with the best metro apps. The package includes five new offerings. For dining, check out "Appetites" to find the best restaurants in town and even make reservations online. For entertainment, it's "Box Seat," your guide to what's on stage or screen. Pretend you're a traffic reporter with "Helicopter," the app that flies you above the city to see road congestion and plan alternate routes. Gaming fun comes from "Marathon Runner" and "Art Prize," both challenging your thumb action with tours through the best of the city. All apps are customizable to the 225 largest cities in the United States.

### Suite #2 – The Napa
Lie back and taste the merlot. The Napa Suite is ripe with game apps—the rich wine-country landscapes of "Vintage," the excitement of "Eco-Warrior," and the high-tech inventions of "Silicon Valley." For a touch of real life, manage your finances with "Billionaire." Who needs a business manager anyway? Finally, let "News Cruise" send podcasts right to your handheld from the best financial news publications and shows—the *Wall Street Journal*, MSNBC, and more than 20 other sources.

### Suite #3 – The Heartland
Here's a suite of apps as hardworking as an Iowa farmer. Manage your small business with "Owner Operator"—accounting spreadsheets, tax forms, and up-to-date alerts about market prices. "Satellite" offers the latest weather information, complete with satellite views updated every 15 minutes. Gamers will flock to "Snow Bird" to negotiate life as a winter resident down south. Then there's "College Courtside." Pick your conference (Big Ten, Missouri Valley, whatever), build a basketball dream team, and hit the hoops online. "News Cruise," with podcasts of the latest business news, is also part of the suite. Like your handheld? We wanna hold your hand!

B. Check (✓) the categories in the chart based on information from the ad.

| | Game Application | Business Management Application | News/Current Conditions Applications |
|---|---|---|---|
| Billionaire | | | |
| Helicopter | | | |
| Vintage | | | |
| News Cruise | | | |
| Owner Operator | | | |
| Snow Bird | | | |

Strategies for taking the:    TOEFL® Test    TOEIC® Test    IELTS™ Test

Understanding numbers is especially hard in listening tests because the information goes by quickly. To prepare, practice reading numbers and listening to them in conversation, on TV, and in other settings.

## 2 Practice with numbers in a reading

Read the software advertisement again. Fill each blank with a number.

1. A Sweet Suite costs ____.
2. The apps in "The Manhattan" contain information about ____ cities.
3. "News Cruise" gets information from more than ____ sources.
4. The satellite views in "The Heartland" are updated every ____ minutes.

## 3 Practice with numbers in speech

AUDIO FILE 🔊 Listen to the radio news report about a conspiracy theory. Circle the letter of the best answer.

1. About how many years before the report was the Brainerd fluoride controversy?
   a. 10    b. 40    c. 70
2. In what year did the Minnesota Legislature pass a law requiring fluoridation?
   a. 1967    b. 1970    c. 1980
3. How much would Minnesotans save on dentist bills if all drinking water was fluoridated?
   a. $7.50    b. $1,455,046    c. $1,455
4. Marge Tollefson says that ____ of people drinking fluoridated water have cancer.
   a. about 17 percent    b. 60 to 70 percent    c. more than 70 percent
5. How old is Harvey Larson?
   a. 26    b. 36    c. 76

## 4 Check your understanding

AUDIO FILE 🔊 Listen to the news report again. Write T for true or F for false.

1. ____ Fluoride was added to water in order to kill living things in the water.
2. ____ The state government would not give fluoride to people in Brainerd.
3. ____ Gus Roper says that many people in the 1970s did not trust the government.
4. ____ Fluoride is now added to the water in Brainerd.

## 5 Skills in review

Look again at "Who's that girl?" on p. 40 of the Workbook. Scan the reading for the numbers. (Hint: Some are spelled out, not in numerals.) Practice pronouncing each of them.

When you listen for numbers, be ready for the word *and* (usually pronounced '*n*') as part of some numbers. For example, the number 650 could be said as "six hundred 'n' fifty.

# Unit 7 | Sentence insertion and pronoun reference

## Organization: where to add sentences

Some reading tests (such as the TOEFL®) include **sentence-insertion** questions. You have to decide where a new sentence would fit best into the reading. Vocabulary and grammar clues in the reading can help you choose.

### 1 Finding the best place for new sentences

A. Read the article.

# The Emptiness of Empty-Nesting

Life for Ron and Joanne Wickham used to be full of soccer games, birthday parties, school plays, and parent-teacher conferences. (A) Now the evenings are empty except for TV, and the weekends seem to last forever. The children whose activities used to fill *their* time have moved away and have left empty spaces. The Wickham parents have what is usually called Empty-Nest Syndrome.

(B) In their mid-50s, they have two children, Anne and Josh. Anne just graduated from California State University-Fullerton and is looking for a banking job in the Bay Area. Josh is still a junior at Claremont McKenna College near Los Angeles, but he can only rarely make the 460-mile trip home to visit his parents. Back in Ukiah, Ron and Joanne often feel the house is too big. "*It* doesn't really echo," says Ron, "but it feels like it should. Where is everybody?"

Empty-nesters everywhere know the feeling. (C) They are typically between the ages of 48 and 60—still working, still involved in their communities, still rooted. *This* means they aren't free to travel for entertainment or to pull up stakes and move elsewhere. Generally, they live in the homes where they raised their children. Their daily routines may still echo their full-nest days, with wake-up times meant for driving kids to school or meals that include the children's favorite foods. (D) "Eventually, a so-called empty nest starts to feel normal and new routines develop," says UCLA psychology professor Jaswant Singh. "Most parents complete this journey just fine, but *it* usually feels pretty lonely."

B. Next to each sentence, write the letter from the article where it would fit best.

1. ____ Ron and Joanne both work for the Heritage Insurance Company in Ukiah, California.

2. ____ Therapists point out that Empty-Nest Syndrome doesn't last forever.

3. ____ For most of the past 20 years, they spent their evenings reminding their children to do homework and helping them complete it.

4. ____ They are entering a new stage of life, but they remain tied to their former stage.

## Pronoun reference

Some test questions focus on **pronoun reference**. You have to understand the noun phrases or ideas that words like *he, it, they,* or *this* refer to. Note that *this, that, these,* or *those* may refer to a larger idea.

Strategies for taking the:   TOEFL® Test   TOEIC® Test   IELTS™ Test

## 2 Understanding pronoun reference in a reading

Read the article again. Notice the pronouns in italics. In the chart, match each one with the noun phrase or idea it refers to. One noun phrase/idea will NOT be used.

| Pronoun | Noun or Phrase Idea |
|---|---|
| 1. ____ *their* (paragraph 1) | a. being tied to a place |
| 2. ____ *It* (paragraph 2) | b. having an empty nest |
| 3. ____ *This* (paragraph 3) | c. Ron and Joanne |
| 4. ____ *it* (paragraph 3) | d. the house |
| | e. the journey |

## 3 Understanding pronoun reference in a lecture

A. AUDIO FILE 🔊 Listen to the lecture. Understand the main ideas. Also, try to listen for what the pronouns refer to.

B. AUDIO FILE 🔊 Listen again to find the answer to each question. Circle the letter.

1. What word/phrase sounds like a reality show?

   a. *good morning*    b. *situation*    c. *celebrity homecoming*

2. For whom was Independence, Missouri, a hometown?
   a. Harry and Bess Truman    b. high circles    c. Churchill and Stalin

3. What did the community feel good about?

   a. the town    b. the presence of the Trumans    c. some inconvenience

4. What did Mellencamp shoot many of his videos in and around?

   a. Seymour    b. his career    c. his roots

5. According to the lecturer, where do people love John Mellencamp?

   a. Seymour    b. Mellencamp Pavilion    c. Bloomington

## 4 Check your understanding

AUDIO FILE 🔊 Listen to the lecture again. Write T for true or F for false.

1. ____ The main idea of the lecture is how people become famous.

2. ____ Both Truman and Mellencamp were musicians.

3. ____ Truman moved back to his hometown because he disliked politics.

4. ____ John Mellencamp provided money for a university sports building.

## 5 Skills in review

Look again at **CD 26** on p. 83 of the Workbook. Find places where the pronoun *it* is used. Try to figure out what *it* means in each case. To check the answer key for this exercise, number the lines in the dialogue from 1 to 37.

> Usually pronouns come after the things they refer to. When you hear the pronoun, think quickly back to find its referent.

# Unit 8 | Graded opposites and superlatives

**Antonyms** (e.g., *cheap/expensive*) are exact opposites. Other words are opposite in some ways but not exactly. These are **graded opposites**. To answer some reading questions, you have to understand the meanings of these words.

**Example of graded opposites: PRICES**

free     cheap     reasonable     expensive     exorbitant

## 1 Understanding graded opposites

A. Read the passage from a textbook.

## The Medieval Warm Period

Climate changes history, and the Medieval Warm Period (MWP) offers the clearest proof in modern history. The MWP stretched **roughly from CE 800 to 1300**, and it draws its name from the warmer sea and air temperatures during that time. Seawater temperatures were at least 1° C (1.8° F) warmer on average than now. Air temperatures over land were probably **about 1.5° C (2.7° F) warmer** than today's. **To be precise**, climatologists know for sure only that these temperatures occurred in the region of the North Atlantic Ocean. This includes the northernmost parts of Europe, Greenland, Iceland, and northeastern North America. It seems very unlikely that the Southern Hemisphere saw such warming. Similarly, evidence from ice cores and tree rings makes it doubtful that warming took place in other parts of the Northern Hemisphere. In fact, this period was one of the coldest in some parts of Asia.

During the MWP, the peoples **broadly known as the Vikings** took advantage of the warmth to reshape history. During the warm period, glaciers and polar ice melted, allowing the societies of northern Europe to flourish. Glaciers in Norway, Greenland, and Iceland retreated, exposing more farmland and allowing forests to expand. On the Scandinavian peninsula, this provided more food and timber for towns and ships. It also enriched and strengthened warlords, the boldest of whom raided overseas targets to get riches and land. In southwestern Greenland, the retreat of the glaciers by **approximately 100 kilometers (62 miles)** allowed the Vikings to set up permanent settlements. Our knowledge of Viking history is relatively good because the Norse kept some of the most detailed records in Europe. Their sagas (tales of heroes) are not totally believable but do tell us a lot. The Icelandic sagas say that the warrior Eric the Red landed **exactly 14 ships of colonists** on Greenland's southwestern coast in CE 985. The number of actual settlers is **impossible to determine**, but estimates run from 2000 to 10,000. A great reduction in ice floating through the Atlantic allowed the Vikings to sail unimpeded not only to Iceland and Greenland but also to Canada and perhaps the northeastern U.S. The sagas say that **in the year 1000**, Eric's son, Leif Ericsson, landed at Vinland in North America. Previous uncertainty about whether the Norse actually reached North America has been dispelled. Archaeological findings at L'Anse aux Meadows in Canada are definitively Norse and date from the MWP.

Strategies for taking the:    TOEFL® Test    TOEIC® Test    IELTS™ Test

B. Give each boldfaced phrase from the reading a number from 0 to 3 to show how exact it is.
Very exact = 3; not exact at all = 0. (Different students may come up with different numbers.)

1. ___ roughly from CE 800 to 1300

2. ___ about 1.5° C (2.7° F) warmer

3. ___ to be precise

4. ___ broadly known as the Vikings

5. ___ approximately 100 kilometers (62 miles)

6. ___ exactly 14 ships of colonists

7. ___ impossible to determine

8. ___ in the year 1000

## Superlatives

**Superlatives** indicate that something is at the extremes. It is the *best*, *least*, *most*, etc. Look for the ending –*est* on short adjectives (*tallest*, *quickest*) and *most* with longer ones (*most beautiful*). A "negative" superlative always includes *least* (*least well-known*).

## 2 Recognizing superlatives in a reading

The reading in Exercise 1 contains five superlative adjectives. One of them is written below. Write the other four on the lines.

*clearest*

_____   _____   _____   _____

## 3 Understanding superlatives in speech

AUDIO FILE 🔊 Listen to the conversation between two friends. Circle the letter of the best answer.

1. What kind of snake kills more people than any other?

   a. the funnel web
   b. the inland taipan
   c. the black mamba

2. Which city is farthest from Washington, D.C.?

   a. Canberra, Australia
   b. Wellington, New Zealand
   c. Punta Arenas, Chile

3. What question do Diego and Maureen disagree about?

   a. What is the closest populated place to Antarctica?
   b. What is the most poisonous spider in the world?
   c. Where is the best museum of Antarctic exploration?

4. According to Diego, what is New Zealand's most important "best?"

   a. its location
   b. its sheep
   c. its rugby team

## 4 Check your understanding

AUDIO FILE 🔊 Listen to the conversation again. Write T for true or F for false.

1. ___ Maureen knows approximately how far Canberra is from Washington.

2. ___ Humans often encounter inland taipan snakes.

3. ___ Diego was born in Chile.

4. ___ The New Zealand rugby team is called the All-Blacks.

> When you listen for superlatives, the -*st* sound is a clue. So is *the*, because almost every superlative includes it.

## 5 Skills in review

Look again at Exercise 8 on p. 52 of the Workbook. Write three sentences using superlatives to describe Dangerman and his work.

# Unit 9 | Multiple meanings and factors/influences

**Understanding which meaning is used**

Test questions may ask you to choose the best meaning of a word in context. For example, does *bank* mean "a place with money" or "the side of a river?" Understanding the context will help you choose.

## 1 Choosing the right meaning

A. Read the article.

## Extreme Memory: The Woman Who Can't Forget

Can you remember what you were doing on January 21, 2006? Was it a Monday, a Tuesday, or what? What was on TV? What did you have for lunch? Jill Price can tell you instantly, without looking it up, without even stopping to think about it. Price can remember the events of every day in her life, from 1980 to the <u>present</u>, in great detail. As Price told TV journalist Diane Sawyer, "If you <u>throw</u> a date <u>out</u> at me, it's as if I pulled a videotape out, put it in a VCR, and just watched the day. As it happened. From my point of view."

Price has a rare condition called hyperthymestic syndrome (HS). This big term has a simple meaning— an automatic memory of nearly everything that happened in her life. She gets clear pictures in her mind of what she did on a certain day, the weather, the day of the week, and any important news she heard on that day. She remembers only things that happened directly to her. Her super-memory is all autobiographical. In other <u>respects</u>, her memory is not especially good. She did not memorize facts very well in school. She can't remember long strings of numbers or entire phone books, as some other people with super-memories can.

Memory specialist Dr. James McGaugh at the University of California-Irvine met Price in 2000 and diagnosed her condition. Since then, only two other persons in the world have been found to have HS. The factors producing her remarkable memory are still not fully understood. By scanning her brain, McGaugh discovered that a part called the amygdala is three times as large as normal. This is almost certainly a factor, but scientists know too little about the brain to say exactly how. Her exceptional memory first appeared just after her family <u>moved</u> from New Jersey to California. Maybe the shock of the move played a part. Her memory became almost perfect when she was 14, at an age when the body's chemistry changes a lot. Maybe there is a chemical cause as well.

Price says her amazing memory is not entirely a good thing. She cannot turn off the memories when they come. Consequently, she is often distracted from important things in her life right now. Also, she remembers bad things as well as good—including painful events she'd rather forget. As Price says, "Every day, you are able to take the trash and put it outside. Well, I've got 43 years of trash that just piles up and follows me around." By the way, January 21, 2006, was a Saturday, and the TV show *Cops* was on from 8:00 to 9:00 in the evening. You can google it to confirm, but Jill Price could tell you a lot faster.

B. Circle the letter of the best answer to each question. The key words in the questions are underlined in the article.

1. Which is closest in meaning to *present* as it is used in the article?

   a. gift      b. now      c. show

2. Which is closest in meaning to *throw out* as it is used in the article?

   a. get rid of      b. give      c. not allow

3. Which is closest in meaning to *respects* as it is used in the article?

   a. ways      b. polite words      c. views of the past

4. Which is closest in meaning to *moved* as it is used in the article?

   a. made a motion or gesture      b. inspired emotion      c. changed location

Strategies for taking the:    TOEFL® Test    TOEIC® Test    IELTS™ Test

Many events or situations are caused by several things, not just one. Test questions may ask about these **factors** or **influences**. It's important to understand what they are and how they work together.

## 2 Recognizing factors and influences

Read the article again. Match each item with a possible factor or influence. Write the letter in the blank.

| Items | Possible Factors/Influences |
|---|---|
| 1. ____ Dr. McGaugh's knowledge of Price's brain | a. reaching the age of 14 |
| 2. ____ chemical changes | b. brain scans |
| 3. ____ distraction | c. automatic memories |
| 4. ____ HS | d. a large amygdala |

## 3 Listening for factors and influences

AUDIO FILE 🔊 Listen to the conversation between two friends. Circle the best phrase to complete each sentence.

1. The need to film in a place big enough for six people caused (Monica's apartment to be unrealistically big / the show to become extremely popular).

2. One reason shows with ensemble casts succeed is that (there is always just one big star / viewers can find a favorite character).

3. Setting many *Friends* scenes in a coffee house helped its popularity because (the characters owned the coffee house / coffee houses were becoming hugely popular at the time).

4. At the end, the cast of *Friends* did not look the same as at the beginning because (they had spouses / they were 10 years older).

## 4 Check your understanding

AUDIO FILE 🔊 Listen to the conversation again. Write T for true or F for false.

1. ____ Chuck and Noriah agree that no good sitcom has appeared since *Friends*.

2. ____ Noriah doesn't like Rachel because everyone else likes her.

3. ____ Some parts of *Friends* were set in an apartment and other parts in a coffee house.

4. ____ *Friends* ended because it was no longer popular.

## 5 Skills in review

Look again at "My family's bad habits" on p. 56 of the Workbook. These words from the exercise have more than one meaning: *leaves*, *combs*, *toast*, and *turn on*. Look in your dictionary and write two definitions for each word—the definition that matches its use in the Workbook and one other definition.

> Keep an open mind about words with many meanings. Think you know the meaning? If your meaning does not match the context, check your dictionary.

## Recognizing statements of danger or risk

A reading passage may point out dangers or risks. Some words that signal this are *warning*, *caution*, *beware*, and *danger*. Less direct signals are verbs of possibility like *could cause*, *may lead to*, *may result in*, etc.

1  **Understanding safety instructions**

A. Read the page from an instruction manual.

## Important! Safety Instructions for Your New Lawn Mower

**Your new BladeWinner lawn mower is a powerful machine. Operate it with care. Please observe the following safety guidelines.**

**1)** For fuel, use only unleaded gasoline. The use of other fuels could result in damage to the engine. Fire is also possible with the use of unauthorized fuels. In case of fire, spray immediately with a Class B fire extinguisher.

**2)** Do not place hands or feet under the mower at any time. Serious injury could result if blades begin turning. If blades must be attended to, follow these steps: (a) move mower to a flat surface, such as a driveway; (b) disconnect spark wire (see diagram); (c) turn mower on its side; (d) wear strong gloves to prevent cuts when examining blades.

**3)** Wear eye protection. The mower's spinning blades can propel small stones, pieces of wood, and other projectiles toward the operator. Protect eyes with wrap-around safety glasses made of shatter-proof plastic.

**4)** Never run the mower over large sticks, rocks, or other obstacles. Damage to the blades may result. Contact with obstacles also increases the chances of injury to the operator.

**5)** Keep small children and pets away from the mower at all times. The mower should never be operated by anyone under 13 years of age.

B. Write the letter of the danger/risk that matches each event/situation.

| Event/Situation | Danger/Risk |
|---|---|
| 1. ____ using fuel other than gasoline | a. blade damage |
| 2. ____ clearing the mower blades | b. cut hands |
| 3. ____ hitting sticks or stones with the mower | c. eye injury |
| 4. ____ mower propelling small stones or sticks | d. fire |

## Understanding how dangers or risks are reduced

A listening or reading passage about dangers probably also mentions how risks can be reduced. Look for statements about ways or methods. Some key words might be *avoid*, *protect*, *keep from*, or *deal with*.

Strategies for taking the:   TOEFL® Test     TOEIC® Test     IELTS™ Test

## 2 Recognizing statements about reducing dangers/risks

Read the manual again. Complete each statement in five words or less.

1. When inspecting the blades, the user can reduce the risk of hand cuts by

   _____ .

2. The danger of eye injury can be reduced by

   _____ .

3. Damage to the blades will be less likely if the operator avoids

   _____ .

## 3 Understanding ways to overcome risks

AUDIO FILE 🔊 Listen to the lecture. Circle the letter of the best answer.

1. What can we do to reduce the risk that large animals will have too little to eat?
   a. protect old forests
   b. make sure new forests replace old ones
   c. break the natural cycle of fires

2. Which of the following reduces the risk of soil losing its richness?
   a. adding ash from wildfires
   b. melting the waxy coating on pine cones
   c. clearing a 100-yard area around a house

3. Which of the following will best keep people from dying in a wildfire?
   a. encouraging them to stay with their property
   b. building houses with fireproof material
   c. evacuating them from the path of the fire

4. What is the most common way in which we now deal with wildfires?
   a. by using firefighters on the ground and planes or helicopters in the air
   b. by preventing people from building houses in areas that have fires
   c. by letting fires burn as part of a natural cycle

## 4 Check Your Understanding

AUDIO FILE 🔊 Listen to the lecture again. Write T for true or F for false.

1. ____ Fires are good because they make room for new plants to grow.

2. ____ The speaker believes people should stay at their houses during a wildfire.

3. ____ The speaker believes people should clear vegetation away from their houses.

4. ____ The safest way to fight a fire is to fly over it and drop water or chemicals.

## 5 Skills in review

Look again at "Water, Water Everywhere!" on pp. 64–65 of the Workbook. Can you think of any dangers involved in exploring space?

> Trust yourself. Using logic, you can imagine how to deal with a risk. Take guesses and check your guesses as you read or listen.

---

*If* clauses: counterfactuals

Some test questions ask about things that did not happen but could have. Recognize **counterfactual** statements by their two parts: (1) an *if* clause; (2) a main clause with *would have*, *could have*, etc.

---

## 1  Understanding counterfactuals

A. Read the article.

# Making Charges: Who Killed the Electric Car?

Car makers have long told this story to Americans: "We don't have the technology to build good electric cars. Customers don't want electrics because they are so unattractive, slow, and hard to charge. We would build them if only people wanted them." Chris Paine casts serious doubt on that story in his hard-hitting documentary film, *Who Killed the Electric Car?* The title suggests a murder mystery, and that's what Paine provides. Well, some of it is a mystery. We know the victim from the start—an electric car called the EV1. Also, we can see that Paine will largely blame the General Motors Corporation (GM).

---

**Who Killed the Electric Car? (2006) Documentary 92 mins. Director: Chris Paine. Plinyminor Productions.**

---

GM built the EV1 because the California Air Resources Board (CARB) ruled that cars in the state had to stop adding pollution to the air. The EV1, being electric, did not burn gasoline or put out any pollution. With technology available in 1990, GM had no trouble producing a car that could go 100 miles on a single charge and could recharge from an ordinary household electrical outlet. Remember the auto companies' claim that they don't have good electric–car technology? If that were true, the EV1 would never have been born. The company made 1000 EV1s and leased them to customers in Southern California. (In a lease, a customer does not own a car but pays to use it for a certain time.)

Because of its anti-pollution rule, CARB was sued by oil companies, car companies, and the federal government. Under such pressure, CARB dropped its rule. No longer needing the EV1 to obey California's rules, GM responded by attacking its own child. The company ran advertisements saying how bad the EV1 was. Company representatives went on TV and radio shows to say it was unreliable. The company wanted to get the cars back and destroy them. The fact that EV1s were leased, not sold, is an important part of Paine's tale. GM still owned every car and could legally take them back. A few of them went to museums, but GM crushed most of them flat. If EV1s had been owned by their drivers, they would probably still be on the road. Many people who drove them loved them. In fact a group of EV1 drivers offered GM $1.8 million to buy a large number of cars and keep them going. GM refused. The company wanted the car to disappear.

Paine's criticisms of the car industry, Washington's close relationships with the oil industry, and California's state government are harsh. Each, he says, played a role in the murder of the EV1. Each has also defended itself in the wake of the film, but Paine's excellent documentary will be hard for them to dismiss.

---

B. Circle the letter of the best answer.

1. Car companies say they would have built electric cars if
   a. states required them.
   b. customers wanted them.
   c. the cars could stop polluting the air.

2. Because the EV1 was really made, which statement is clearly untrue?
   a. CARB made rules to reduce pollution in California.
   b. The technology for making electric cars doesn't exist.
   c. GM wanted to take the cars back and destroy them.

Strategies for taking the:  TOEFL® Test   TOEIC® Test   IELTS™ Test

3. If EV1 drivers ____ their cars, the vehicles might still be in use.

   a. had leased

   b. had driven

   c. had owned

## 2 Check your understanding

Read the movie review again. Check (✓) each true statement.

1. ☐ Chris Paine works for General Motors.

2. ☐ GM built the EV1 in order to obey rules about air pollution.

3. ☐ Many people bought EV1s when they became available.

4. ☐ Chris Paine believes several groups played roles in the murder of the EV1.

**Understanding what did / didn't happen**

Reading/listening passages mention many events—some that happened, and others that didn't happen. To answer test questions about this, use logic and context. Ask yourself, in this context, what is most likely to be true?

## 3 Practice recognizing what happened

Listen to the press conference. In each set of statements, two are true and one is false. Cross out the false one.

1. Set 1

   a. SunSails put a space-sailing vehicle into orbit.

   b. The space sail was inside a capsule on a rocket.

   c. The rocket did not go far enough to release the space sail.

2. Set 2

   a. SunSails has not yet found the rocket that fell.

   b. The rocket caused some damage in Canada.

   c. The rocket was made in Russia.

3. Set 3

   a. In this launch, SunSails wanted the space-sailing vehicle to stay near Earth.

   b. The space-sailing vehicle is controlled electronically by people on Earth.

   c. SunSails already has a space-sailing vehicle traveling through the solar system.

4. Set 4

   a. Light puts pressure on a space sail and pushes it forward.

   b. A space-sailing vehicle is pushed along by solar wind.

   c. A space sail's speed should increase as it travels through the solar system.

## 4 Check your understanding

AUDIO FILE 🔊 Listen to the press conference again. Write T for true or F for false.

1. ____ The rocket carrying the space sail was launched from the United States.

2. ____ Space sails could travel to the edge of our solar system and even farther.

3. ____ Solar wind is made of light.

4. ____ After the sail gets far from the sun it will need other light to keep going.

How do speakers "get real?" They might say *actually*, *in reality*, or *but really* to indicate that something really happened.

## 5 Skills in review

AUDIO FILE 🔊 Listen again to the press conference. Then look again at the "Wishes and regrets" section on pp. 68–69 of the Workbook. Pretend you are the SunSails spokesperson. What regrets would you have? What wishes?

# Unit 12 | Definitions and the purpose of a statement

## Recognizing definitions in a reading

The answers to some vocabulary questions are given directly in a reading. Phrases like *which means*, *in other words*, or *that is* could introduce a definition. Synonyms can also give definitions.

## 1 Definitions

A. Read the selection from a textbook.

## The Jungle City of Fordlandia

Henry Ford was enormously rich and powerful. His Ford Motor Company was the largest car-maker in the world. It sold more than a million cars each year, mostly its hugely popular Model T. But Ford Motor took some big risks in 1927. Its new River Rouge Assembly Plant in Dearborn, Michigan, the largest factory in the world, was ready to come on line—which in those days meant "start to produce." Ford retired the Model T and dedicated "the Rouge" to building a new, more luxurious Model A—quieter, smoother, and more comfortable.

But Henry Ford was concerned about rubber, which the Model A would need. A quiet car needs good seals (that is, long rubber pads) around the doors and windows. To ride smoothly, it needs good rubber tires. Unfortunately, the United States produced no rubber at all. The world's supply came mostly from British or Dutch companies with Southeast Asian rubber plantations (large farms growing only one crop). Ford worried that, in times of war or trouble, these companies might refuse to sell to Americans. How could the Rouge survive if its rubber supply were cut off?

In typical fashion, Henry Ford devised a big solution for a big problem. After negotiating with the leaders of the South American nation of Brazil, he announced that he would build his own rubber kingdom, called Fordlandia, in jungles near the Amazon River. All the materials for Fordlandia's buildings came by ship from Dearborn, up the Amazon, and then up a smaller river called the Tapajos. By late 1928, Ford's workers had assembled an American town in the tropics and had planted thousands of rubber trees. Yet, Ford wanted more from Fordlandia than just rubber. He was a utopian thinker, that is, someone interested in setting up a perfect society. That is why he told his American managers and Brazilian workers what to eat, what to wear, what times to work, and how to have fun on weekends. He never visited Brazil, but his presence loomed large over Fordlandia.

His experiment eventually failed. Fordlandia's rubber trees produced very little latex (a milky substance from which rubber is produced) because the American planters did not know how to avoid tree diseases. Henry Ford's utopian ideas clashed with the cultures of Fordlandia's Brazilian workers. For example, Ford's ideas of healthy eating—such as brown rice and canned peaches—were so hated by the workers that once they rioted and destroyed the cafeteria. By 1934, Ford was trying to grow rubber in a different location called Belterra, and the failed utopia of Fordlandia was being overgrown by jungle vines.

B. Write a definition or explanation for each word or phrase.

1. assembly plant: _____
2. come on line: _____
3. latex: _____
4. plantation: _____
5. seal: _____
6. utopian: _____

Strategies for taking the: TOEFL® Test   TOEIC® Test   IELTS™ Test

Test questions may ask about the purpose of a statement. Does a writer/
speaker mention something to give examples, introduce a topic, or make a joke?

## 2   Practice with purpose

Read the textbook selection again. Write the letter of the purpose that each mentioned item serves.

| Mentioned Item | Purpose |
|---|---|
| 1. ____ seals and tires | a. examples of the Model A's needs<br>B. examples of what the Rouge produced |
| 2. ____ launch of the Model A | a. explanation of Henry Ford's power<br>b. explanation of Ford's 1927 risk |
| 3. ____ "a big solution to a big problem" | a. introduction to rubber-supply problems<br>b. introduction to founding of Fordlandia |

## 3   Understanding the purpose of statements in speech

AUDIO FILE 🔊 Listen to the conversation between a student and a history professor. Circle the letter
of the best answer.

1. The professor says, "I don't remember your name," in order to
   a. tell Marta that he doesn't have time to talk.
   b. find out Marta's name.
   c. say that he doesn't know the answer to her question.

2. The student mentions Cuba, India, and South Africa in order to name places
   a. that she heard Churchill served as a soldier.
   b. that were part of the British Empire.
   c. that she visited while studying Churchill.

3. The professor mentions the Nobel Prize in order to
   a. give an example of something that's not true about Churchill.
   b. give evidence that Churchill really was a great writer.
   c. give the reason why Churchill is famous now.

4. The student mentions quotations from Churchill because
   a. the professor has mentioned a lot of them in class.
   b. she wants to write about them for an assignment.
   c. she is not sure whether he said everything he is credited with.

## 4   Check your understanding

AUDIO FILE 🔊 Listen to the conversation again. Write T for true or
F for false.

1. ____ Winston Churchill was a prime minister.

2. ____ Churchill was a soldier in Sudan but not in other places.

3. ____ Because Churchill had servants, he never did any hard work.

2. ____ The professor says that Churchill used the phrase, "blood, toil,
   tears, and sweat."

> Trying to find
> definitions in a reading?
> Scanning can be a big help.
> Look for parentheses ( ),
> dashes (—), and commas (,).

## 5   Skills in review

Look again at Exercise 4 on p. 77 of the Workbook. Now, look again at the second
paragraph of the Fordlandia reading. Underline the articles, determiners, and
demonstratives in that paragraph. You should underline 11 words.

# Answer Key

## Unit 1 (pp. 2–3)

**1** 1. a;  2. c;  3. b

**2** Check (✔) 1 and 3

**3** Check (✔) Ted 2 and 3; Lucia 4 and 6; Mari 7 and 9

**4** 1. F; 2. T;  3. T;  4. T

**5** Answers will vary.

## Unit 2 (pp. 4–5)

**1** Check (✔): 1. to get advice about what to do; 2. selling toys that contain lead; 3. not having to pay $800 a day; 4. not being able to reach an English speaker

**2** 1. F; 2. T; 3. F; 4. F

**3** 1. c; 2. a; 3. a; 4. b

**4** I just talked <u>to</u> Jim Decker <u>at</u> the San Francisco office. The issue is a shipment <u>of</u> toys now <u>on</u> the docks <u>in</u> S.F. Apparently, we've got three shipping containers there, but Jim doesn't want to sign <u>for</u> them because there's a problem <u>with</u> the paperwork. The shipper did not send a certification that the toys are lead-free. As you know, Seebolt policy is really strict <u>about</u> that, and Jim doesn't want to take a chance. We definitely don't want to sell any toys <u>with</u> lead <u>in</u> them. We could land <u>in</u> court, and more importantly, we would never, ever want to sell dangerous toys.

However, NOT signing could have serious costs. We've never had any trouble <u>with</u> this manufacturer—never any lead, always good quality, etc. If we refuse the shipment, we could lose a good supplier. If the shipment is really OK and we let it stay <u>on</u> dock <u>for</u> a long time, we'd have to pay storage fees <u>at</u> $800 per day! Jim has been trying <u>for</u> a whole day to reach the supplier but can't get through <u>to</u> anyone <u>in</u> management. Apparently, he can't even get through to anyone who speaks English. I told Jim I'd bring it up <u>to</u> you. What's your advice? Should he risk it and sign? Thanks <u>in</u> advance <u>for</u> your help.

## Unit 3 (pp. 6–7)

**1** 1. a; 2. b;  3. a

**2** Check (✔) 2

**3** 1. T; 2. T; 3. F; 4. F

**4** 1. e; 2. f;  3. c;  4. a; 5. d;  6. b

**5** Answers will vary.

## Unit 4 (pp. 8–9)

**1** This exercise is subjective, so answers will vary. Possible answers explained: A. 3 The context ridicules the "alien" explanation strongly but then expresses some sympathy for early believers.; B. 4 The writer is unfailingly negative and scornful in this sentence.; C. 1 The writer grants some credibility by calling the hypothesis "a little less goofy."; D. 2 The writer is straightforward about this explanation being doubtful, but no strong words of contempt are used.

**2** Check (✔) 1 and 3

**3** 1. b; 2. c; 3. b

**4** 1. T; 2. F; 3. F; 4. T

**5** Answers will vary. Possible answers: People accepted Abagnale as a pilot because he had a uniform and a fake ID card. They accepted him as a lawyer because he had a fake degree from Harvard and knew a lot about the law from studying for an exam.

## Unit 5 (pp. 10–11)

**1** 1. b; 2. a; 3. c

**2** 1. T; 2. F; 3. F; 4. T

**3** 1. scheduled exams; 2. flexible; 3. talk to her professors; 4. grade; 5. lose her scholarship; 6. advisor

**4** Answers will vary.

**5** Answers will vary.

## Unit 6 (pp. 12–13)

**1** Game Applications: SnowBird, Vintage; Business Management Applications: Billionaire, Owner Operator; News/Current Conditions Applications: Helicopter, News Cruise

**2** 1. $24.99; 2. 225; 3. 20; 4. 15

**3** 1. b; 2. a; 3. b; 4. c; 5. a

**4** 1. F; 2. F; 3. T; 4. T

**5** Answers will vary.

## Unit 7 (pp. 14–15)

**1** 1. B; 2. D; 3. A; 4. C

**2** 1. c; 2. d; 3. a; 4. e

**3** 1. c; 2. a; 3. b; 4. a; 5. c

**4** 1. F; 2. F; 3. F; 4. T

**5** Answers will vary. Possible answers:
Line 6: the thing that is upsetting you
Line 11: his criticism
Line 17: his behavior
Line 26: that he loves me
Line 27: that he loves you

## Unit 8 (pp. 16–17)

**1** Answers will vary. Suggested answers: 1. 1 or 2; 2. 1 or 2; 3. 3; 4. 1 or 2; 5. 1 or 2; 6. 3; 7. 0; 8. 3

**2** northernmost, coldest, boldest, most detailed

**3** 1. c; 2. a; 3. a; 4. c

**4** 1. T; 2. F; 3. F; 4. T

**5** Answers will vary. Possible answers:  Dangerman takes some of the greatest risks in the filming business. Dangerman has survived some of the worst weather on Earth. Dangerman has been to the coldest town on Earth.

## Unit 9 (pp. 18–19)

**1** 1. b; 2. b; 3. a; 4. c

**2** 1. b;  2. a; 3. c; 4. d

**3** 1. Monica's apartment to be unrealistically big; 2. viewers can find a favorite character; 3.  coffee houses were becoming hugely popular at the time;  4. they were 10 years older

**4** 1. T; 2. F; 3. T; 4. F

**5** Answers will vary. Possible answers:
*leaves* – WB: "lets something be in a condition even after he goes away" Other: "goes away"
*combs* – WB: "to arrange hair with a toothed device" Other: "to look carefully through something"
*toast* – WB: "bread that has been slightly browned by heat" Other: "a drink accompanied by nice words about someone"
*turn on* – WB: "start an electrical device" Other: "suddenly go against someone you had once treated nicely"

## Unit 10 (pp. 20–21)

**1** 1. d;  2. b; 3. a;  4. c

**2** Answers will vary. Possible answers: 1. wearing gloves; 2. wearing safety glasses; 3. running the mower over stones (or large sticks)

**3** 1. b; 2. a; 3. c; 4. a

**4** 1. T; 2. F; 3. T; 4. F

**5** Answers will vary.

## Unit 11 (pp. 22–23)

**1** 1 b; 2. b; 3. c

**2** Check (✓) 2 and 4

**3** Cross out: Set 1, a; Set 2, b; Set 3, c; Set 4, b

**4** 1. F; 2. T;  3. F;  4. T

**5** Answers will vary.

## Unit 12 (pp. 24–25)

**1** 1 Answers will vary. Possible answers: 1. a factory; 2. start to produce; 3. a milky substance from which rubber is produced; 4. a large farm growing only one crop; 5. a long rubber pad; 6. related to setting up a perfect society

**2** 1. a; 2. b; 3. b

**3** 1. b; 2. a; 3. b; 4. c

**4** 1. T; 2. F; 3. F; 4. T

**5** But Henry Ford was concerned about rubber, which <u>the</u> Model <u>A</u> would need. <u>A</u> quiet car needs good seals (<u>that</u> is, long rubber pads) around <u>the</u> doors and windows. To ride smoothly, it needs good rubber tires. Unfortunately, <u>the</u> United States produced <u>no</u> rubber at all. <u>The</u> world's supply came mostly from British or Dutch companies with Southeast Asian rubber plantations (large farms growing only <u>one</u> crop). Ford worried that, in times of war or trouble, <u>these</u> companies might refuse to sell to Americans.  How could <u>the</u> Rouge survive if <u>its</u> rubber supply were cut off?

# Audio Scripts

## Unit 1

T = Ted  L = Lucia  M = Mariya

**T:** I'm Ted, from San Diego, California….uh….My strongest childhood memory is about a place called Children's Pool. It's up in La Jolla, a suburb kind of north and west of the city. To get there, my brothers and I had to take a city bus from downtown and ride it to the middle of La Jolla. From there we could just walk down to the shore of the ocean. The Children's Pool is really just part of the ocean, where a long sea wall protects part of the beach from big waves. At that time, in the 1990s, kids shared the beach with these great little seal pups. So, it's like, we're swimming, and we keep bumping up against these fat little animals in the water. It was really fun. I guess they don't let kids use the Children's Pool anymore because there are so many seals now.

**L:** Hi, I'm Lucia, from a city in Brazil called Santarém. My strongest childhood memory is of a place in my town called "the wedding of the waters." We've got two rivers in town, the Amazon and the Tapajós. They look totally different. The Amazon, which is the biggest and most powerful river in the whole world, has a milky light-brown color. That's because it carries soil all the way from the Andes Mountains, like more than two thousand miles away. The Tapajós looks totally different, a really dark blue. Further east it all mixes in and is just the Amazon, but where they meet, where they have their "wedding," half of the river is brown and half is blue. It's great to look at, but you have to be careful. If you fall in the water, you could get carried away. And you wouldn't believe the stuff you see in the river. Every day you see a couple of whole trees from the jungle float by. Once I even saw a house floating away in the brown part of the water.

**M:** Hi. I'm Mariya. I'm from Athens, Greece, which I'm sure you've heard of because it is super-important in history. My strongest memory from childhood is when my family used to take a train from the middle of Athens up to a suburb called Kifissia. You had to get off the train there because it's the last station, the end of the line. It's a kind of rich place, where lots of powerful Greek families live, but people from all over Athens go there for fun on weekends. My family…we would get off at the train station right in the square and then have a little lunch. Then we liked to take a taxi up to a beautiful green mountainside, the Penteli mountain. We hiked around, and I remember the smell of pines and the beautiful cool breezes. It's really sad, because in 1995 a huge fire burned up a lot of those forests.

## Unit 2

Gold was discovered in California in January 1848 by James W. Marshall. He was part-owner, with John Sutter, of a new sawmill on a fast-flowing stream, called the American River, in north-central California. To make water flow better as it turned the mill's machinery, he was trying to deepen the channel for it. Then he noticed two yellowish rocks. With his basic knowledge of minerals, he knew that they were either a sulfur-iron combination or gold. He pounded the stones between two heavier rocks. The mineral did not break but could be hammered flat. It had to be gold.

News of the find reached the eastern United States—and many other nations—within a few months. The story said that gold could easily be found, without special equipment. A miner only had to put river-bottom sand in a pan, swish it around, and pick out the gold. Through the next year, 1849, more than 300,000 "49ers" rushed to California to find their fortunes. Most of them had no idea of the trouble that lay ahead.

About half of the 49ers traveled to California by land. At that time, before 1868, there was no railroad across the country. A land trip to California typically meant at least three months of great hardships. Would-be miners crossed the Great Plains by foot or wagon, then climbed the steep slopes over the Rocky Mountains. Then they walked through deadly deserts in Utah, Nevada, or, less commonly, Arizona. Finally they went over the rugged, snowy Sierra Nevada Mountains on California's eastern border. Along most of the way, they risked attack by American Indians trying to protect their territory from the land-hungry U.S. government.

The other half came by sea. Typically, they boarded ships at New York or another eastern port, sailed south along South America's Atlantic coast, went around the constantly stormy Cape Horn, and then headed north to San Francisco. This usually took about eight months. Indian attacks were not an issue, but other hazards—like seasickness, shipboard disease, and a lack of food or fresh water—might await. To shorten the trip, some 49ers got off their ships at Panama, fought their way through the jungle to the Pacific, and then caught a different ship heading north. This took a lot less time, but most Panama travelers caught malaria or yellow fever. Many finally arrived in California too sick and weak to go looking for gold.

## Unit 3

O = Officer  W1 = Witness 1
W2 = Witness 2  W3 = Witness 3

**O:** So, how did you happen to see this incident?

**W1:** Well, Officer, it's like this. I'm riding my bike through the neighborhood. About a year ago, I started taking shortcuts through the alleys behind buildings. While I'm going behind the mini-mall, where the jewelry store is, I see a pick-up truck parked there.

**O:** What kind of truck?

**W1:** Well, I'm not sure. A light-colored one. This looks a little strange to me, so I stop and look around. I see a guy wearing a tan-colored work coat and a baseball cap trying to get the back door open. As I watch him, I pull out my cell phone and dial 911. Just then, he turns and sees me. I'm thinking, what if he has a gun? So I ride away as fast as I can.

**O:** You saw something happening at the jewelry store. Why don't you tell me about it?

**W2:** It was really scary. I was walking past the windows of the jewelry store. I had just come out of the card shop right next door. The jewelry store had already closed for the day, but I noticed a small area of light moving around inside. I knew right away it was a flashlight. I'm thinking, why would anyone be shining a flashlight in the jewelry store? I froze because I knew something was wrong. So I just stood there a minute and watched. Just as I saw the light shine on a jewelry case, a hammer came down on it and shattered the glass. This guy started grabbing earrings and necklaces and all sorts of stuff. Then I ran back into the card shop and told them to call the police.

**O:** Tell me about the jewelry store. What did you see?

**W3:** Well, first I heard something. Oh yeah…I was going back to my car. About fifteen minutes earlier, I realized that I had left my wallet in the car, and I'm like… "Whoa! Not a good thing." So…

**O:** Get back to what you saw.

**W3:** OK. Sorry. I heard a loud sound, like something falling. So I hurried around to the back of the mini-mall. When I got to the alley, I saw a gym bag down on the ground and a guy trying to scoop jewelry into it. My first reaction was to go and help the guy, but as I started walking toward him I realized, "Uh-oh. This isn't right." I shouted, "Hey. What's going on over there?" Maybe that wasn't so smart. The guy stood up, and while he was looking straight at me, he reached inside his coat. I don't know if he was going for a gun or knife or what, but I ran out to the main street. About 30 seconds later, I heard the truck in the alley start up and roar away, real fast.

## Unit 4

T = Tina  F = Fred

**T:** Not that I really believe in this stuff, but did you see this story about the haunted dorm?

**F:** You're kidding, right?

**T:** No. Seriously. The student newspaper says, "Paranormal Researchers Find Ghost in Ford Hall." Students over there are really scared.

**F:** How could they find a ghost? There's no such thing as ghosts.

**T:** Well, the dorm director hired a ghost research company. They set up, like, security cameras in the laundry room, and when they looked at the recording, they saw a white shape in the corner. Then it moved back and forth through the room.

**F:** Laundry room? Ha! Somebody probably got wrapped up in a sheet.

**T:** And the recording showed that each time the ghost passed someone, the student reacted, like looked around or acted cold or something.

**F:** That doesn't prove anything.

**T:** Well, also, they found the elevator going up and down for no reason. Nobody touched the buttons, but suddenly the elevator moved between floors.

**F:** So? Must be some electrical problem. None of this is very convincing.

**T:** I'm just telling you what the article says. I don't believe in ghosts either, really. But then, you've got to admit Ford Hall is kind of a creepy place.

**F:** It's just old, like from the 1800s.

**T:** I heard that back in the seventies, a student died there. And they say he died…IN THE LAUNDRY ROOM!

**F:** Tina! Come on! You're not falling for this stuff, are you?

**T:** No…but…there's all this evidence. The white shape, the dead guy in the seventies….

**F:** That's just a rumor. I'm going to google that later.

**T:** Another thing—these researchers recorded a spooky voice in the laundry room. It sounds like someone saying, "Get out! Get out!"

**F:** Yeah. It was probably a washing machine that needs some oil.

## Unit 5

J = Jen    B = Brad

**J:** Well, Brad, it looks like I'll have to miss my sister's wedding. It's on May 12th, and I have three final exams that day.

**B:** That's terrible, Jen. Your sister will feel really awful about that.

**J:** Yeah, I know. You don't have to remind me.

**B:** Isn't there some way around this? Can't you ask the professors to give your exams on some other day?

**J:** The problem is, all of them said at the beginning of the semester that there will be no alternate exam dates—and no make-ups. I'd be embarrassed to ask any of them.

**B:** Well, maybe they can make exceptions for you. You have a good reason.

**J:** Hmmm. I don't know.

**B:** You could always just take a grade of "incomplete" in those classes. You know, carry an "I" until you have a chance to take the exams later.

**J:** For three classes? I'm only taking four. That would mean I get only one real grade for this semester. I bet I'd lose my scholarship.

**B:** OK. This is a big problem. I think you need some help. You should go talk to your academic advisor.

**J:** I don't know what she could do about it. She just helps people plan their courses.

**B:** No, they can do more than that. Maybe she could write letters to the professors of those classes, you know, requests for some flexibility in the exam schedule.

**J:** I see what you mean.

## Unit 6

N = News anchor         TB = Tammy Barnes
MT = Marge Tollefson    BH = Bill Harmon
VS = Vern Sundstrom     HJ = Hetty James

**N:** About 40 years ago, the Minnesota city of Brainerd buzzed with talk of a conspiracy. HBP Radio correspondent Tammy Barnes visited Brainerd this week to see whether the great water conspiracy of the 1970s still lives in northern Minnesota.

**TB:** At issue was fluoride, a natural chemical found in most water on Earth. The American Dental Association, the U.S. surgeon general, and the Minnesota State Legislature agreed that cities should put more fluoride in their drinking water to prevent tooth decay. The citizens of Brainerd disagreed. Marge Tollefson remembers how angry her neighbors were in the early 1970s.

**MT:** It's our water. *We* have to drink it. The government has no right to tell us what to put into it. That's what a lot of people thought. I kinda agreed with them.

**TB:** In 1967, the Minnesota State Legislature passed a law requiring every city to fluoridate its water. They had a lot of evidence on their side. Many studies had shown that higher fluoride levels definitely meant healthier teeth, which meant much lower bills for dental work. It was estimated that, over the course of 10 years, the people of Minnesota would save $1,455,046 on dentist bills if they drank fluoridated water. The cost of fluoridation was low, about $7.50 per person over an entire lifetime. Bill Harmon of Minnesotans for Healthy Teeth.

**BH:** You just can't argue with the research. We have data stretching all the way back to the 1920s. Fluoride protects teeth, and it has no bad side effects.

**TB:** But that's not how many residents of Brainerd saw it. They believed someone was conspiring to wreck their health, take away their rights, or even control their minds. Vern Sundstrom runs an auto dealership in Brainerd.

**VS:** You gotta wonder, why do dentists support this if it's gonna take business away from them? It doesn't make sense. I think they were talking about this big benefit when really that fluoride stuff would rot our teeth in the long term.

**TB:** Indeed, a protest letter from the time said, "A national conspiracy of some kind is aimed at getting the substance into water and such action amounts to giving people medicine against their will. Every town has its fluoride pusher assigned by the American Dental Association." Other Brainerd opponents of fluoridation worried about bigger problems.

**MT:** I read somewhere that fluoridation leads to cancer. Like maybe 75 to 80 percent of people who drink that stuff got some sort of cancer. The doctors wanted us all to get sick so they could make money treating us.

**TB:** Hetty James is with the American Doctors League.

**HJ:** Uh…I just don't know how to respond to that. Almost everyone in the United States drinks fluoridated water. If more than 70 percent of them had cancer, our streets would be empty. Our whole economy would shut down because almost everyone would be sick. I can't see how anyone could believe that.

**TB:** But perhaps the strangest conspiracy theory said that the government was putting mind-control drugs into water along with fluoride. Gus Roper was a community activist in the Seventies. He notes that distrust of the government ran high at that point in history, weakened by the Vietnam War and the Watergate scandal. In the end, the government won the fluoridation battle. Five members of the Brainerd City Council were charged with contempt of court for blocking fluoridation. They changed their minds and Brainerd's water became fluoridated on February 7, 1980. But some residents of Brainerd are still unhappy. Brainerd resident Harvey Larson is only 26 years old, not yet born when the controversy first raged. He says he never drinks the water because he thinks it makes people less intelligent. His evidence? "Look at all the kids who can't do anything but play video games," he says. From Brainerd, Minnesota, I'm Tammy Barnes for HBP Radio.

## Unit 7

I'd like to concentrate today on a situation I call the Celebrity Homecoming. Hey, that sounds like some kind of reality show, I guess, but…seriously, what happens when a local kid goes away, becomes famous, and then comes back to his or her old surroundings? Like consider Harry S. Truman, who was president of the United States from 1945 to 1953. Now, Truman traveled in high circles during his public life, worked with leaders like Churchill and Stalin, but after he left the presidency, he and his wife, Bess, returned to their old hometown of Independence, Missouri. Truman didn't exactly step out of national politics—when you think about it, how could anyone ever just turn off an exciting role like he had—but he enjoyed some privacy and happily kept in touch with the life he knew before the pressures of the presidency. How did the town like having him back? Just fine by most accounts. I'm sure it involved some inconvenience, but, in general, the community felt good about it.

Now, I'm sure I'm going to sound really old to you with my next example, but, let's face it, I am! Anyway, a musician named John Mellencamp became a big deal in the 1980s and 1990s. He came from a little town in Indiana called Seymour, and throughout his career he has often made reference to his small-town roots. He shot many of his music videos in and around it—and, by the way, those were some of the earliest videos that MTV ever played. He could live anywhere he wants, but he and his family have settled back in Indiana, near the college town of Bloomington, where people routinely see him at basketball games and in local restaurants. They love him there, and he has put a lot of money into the place. For example, the Indiana University Hoosiers play basketball in the John Mellencamp Pavilion.

## Unit 8

D = Diego        M = Maureen

**D:** Here's a question for you, Maureen. Let's say you could go on a three-month vacation to any country on Earth. Where would you go?

**M:** I don't know, Diego. I never really thought…Well, that's not true. I HAVE thought about it. Australia and New Zealand. Together.

**D:** I asked about one country. Just one.

**M:** Too bad. If I went that far, I'd go to both. There aren't many places farther away than that.

**D:** What about Antarctica?

**M:** I mean populated places. I looked it up once. Canberra, Australia, is the national capital farthest away from Washington, D.C.—just under 10,000 miles by air—and Wellington, New Zealand, is the next farthest.

**D:** Uh…it's kind of nerdy that you know that, Maureen.

**M:** You know me. I'm a travel freak. If you put Australia and New Zealand together, you get some real extremes.

**D:** I don't know a lot about it, but I know Australia has a lot of poisonous animals—spiders, snakes, things like that.

**M:** True. It's got the most poisonous snake in the whole world. The inland tai… tai…something. Taipan, inland taipan.

**D:** Yeah.

**M:** But I guess some snakes in India or Africa kill more people because humans just don't encounter inland taipans very often.

**D:** I know for sure that the black mamba in Africa kills the most people. And that Australian funnel web spider is the most poisonous in the world too, isn't it? I've got a friend in Sydney who says they used to build webs on the side of his garage.

**M:** You mentioned Antarctica. Wellington, New Zealand is closer to Antarctica than any other capital city. And they've got a museum in Christchurch about Antarctic exploration.

**D:** Hey. That's not fair to Chile. My grandparents came from Chile, and I know it's closer. And what about the Falklands?

**M:** Well, yeah, you can find closer places, but there aren't any big cities or anything.

**D:** Punta Arenas? That's a city. So you talk up New Zealand, I hear they've got a lot of sheep, too. Like 20 sheep for each human?

**M:** No, no. That's a myth. More like 8 or 9 per person, but you shouldn't get this image of sheep all over the place. Are there cows all over the U.S.? Now the Falklands…there's sheep for you.

**D:** Don't tell me you know how many sheep per capita there are in the Falklands.

**M:** Yep. Fifteen. The most in the world.

**D:** Like I said…nerdy. The most important thing about New Zealand is that they've got the best rugby team in the universe. Go All-Blacks!

## Unit 9

**C = Chuck        N = Noriah**

**C:** You know, Noriah, ever since *Friends* ended, there haven't been any good TV sitcoms.

**N:** What about…? Uh…Maybe you're right, Chuck. I can't think of any. Why do you think that is?

**C:** *Friends* was just really special. But why? I guess there were lots of factors. The ensemble approach was just brilliant.

**N:** What's that?

**C:** Ensemble. A group of actors working together. *Friends* didn't have one star, it had six. Everyone who watched it could find a favorite character. Like, Chandler was my man. Not too serious, kind of goofy.

**N:** I know it's really corny to like Rachel, but I admit it. She was smart and beautiful—what great hair!

**C:** I don't know how much you know about the history of sitcoms, but most of the really successful shows had ensembles— *Seinfeld, Cheers, The Office*. You could always find a character you liked.

**N:** But for *Friends* I think it was more than that. The setting was perfect, really appealing to people in their 20s or 30s.

**C:** Right. Monica's apartment was cool and funky—although I don't know how anybody could afford a place that big in Manhattan with….

**N:** Well, it's not really fair to criticize it. There's a practical reason. They had to film in a place big enough for six people.

**C:** Yeah, I know. Central Perk, the coffee house, was a little bit easier to believe.

**N:** That's another reason it really appealed to young people. Coffee houses were just starting to be a big thing back when *Friends* started, some time in the 90s.

**C:** 1994. The coffee house business just became huge at that time.

**N:** Yeah. I don't know if it was coincidence, or if maybe *Friends* helped make it happen.

**C:** Totally believable.

**N:** I wish it was still on. I wonder why they took it off. It was still popular.

**C:** I'm sure there were a lot of reasons. Mostly… think of it, the charm was that these goofy young people with a lot of free time hang out together. By 2004, when it ended, those actors were 10 years older than at the start. Harder to look young and hip.

**N:** That makes sense. Also, the characters were getting married and everything. At the start, they had all these ex-spouses, and even kids, but they acted free and could just be… well… friends.

**C:** Very true. The relationships got complex. And all the actors probably wanted to move on to other things. A lot of them have had successful movie careers since the show ended. No actor wants to play the same character forever.

## Unit 10

Fire is part of nature in the western United States, from the Rocky Mountains westward. Strange as it may seem to you, many experts in forestry and ecology say we should just accept fires. They say we shouldn't fight them. Tampering with nature's cycles, they say, we risk throwing ecosystems off balance. Well, I agree to some extent. Then again, I ask myself whether it's realistic to say, "Let the fires burn."

OK, here's why fires are good. They clear dead vegetation out of forests and grasslands so new plants have room to grow. Letting old forests go unburned can also harm wildlife because they don't produce enough low-hanging leaves or berries to feed large animals. Wildfires also help prevent soil from losing its richness. You'd never guess it by looking at a blackened forest floor right after a fire. It looks dead. But all that ash eventually fertilizes the soil so it's really rich for the new plants that will grow there. And finally, some types of trees can't reproduce without fire. Monterey pines and lots of other conifers produce cones that are covered in a waxy substance. Seeds are released from the cone only if the heat of a fire melts the wax.

So, shouldn't we just let fire do its job? Unfortunately, we can't. Like it or not, much of the West is now full of people. They're not going to abandon their expensive houses and land so that fire can follow its natural cycle. Maybe they should have been smarter and not put their homes in the likely path of a fire. But it's too late for that. The people are there, and they have to be protected. To do so, the government usually orders people to evacuate— to get out—if a fire is coming, but that's not enough. Some people think it's brave to stay with their property through a fire, so they refuse to go.

Other steps are necessary. The best way to eliminate fire risk is to take out all the bushes, trees, and grass near your home. Create a clear space about 100 yards wide. The fire has nothing to burn, so it bypasses your house. However, a lot of people moved to the West specifically to enjoy trees and other vegetation. They refuse to create that clear space. You can also build your house with material that doesn't burn. That's right. There's a thing called autoclaved aerated concrete that can survive a fire of 2000 degrees Fahrenheit. Some houses have been built with it, but so far it hasn't become popular. It's actually a smart idea—fireproof houses—but not perfect. The house itself might be OK in a fire, but everything inside it, including people, will burn. So we usually deal with wildfires in the most expensive and dangerous way possible—a bunch of firefighters on the ground battle a wildfire while planes and helicopters dump water and chemicals from above. Of course, the firefighters are in great danger of getting caught by a fire that changes direction. Planes and helicopters are in great danger of crashing because of the swirling winds above a fire.

So we're left with a system that's terrible. And we risk being stuck with it for a long time to come. We can break out of it if we convince western homeowners to be smarter about fire safety, but I don't think that's going to happen.

## Unit 11

**S = Spokesperson        R1 = Reporter 1        R2 = Reporter 2**

**S:** Thank you for coming, ladies and gentlemen. As you know, SunSails is leading a project to put a ship into outer space that can sail for great distances powered by light from the sun. Yesterday we conducted a launch from an island in the Barents Sea off the north coast of Russia. Our launch vehicle was a Russian-made Spotsaya rocket; it carried a space-sailing vehicle in a pressurized capsule. The rocket did, in fact, reach the upper limits of Earth's atmosphere. However, we are disappointed to report that it failed to reach an altitude where it could orbit Earth and release the sail.

**R1:** What happened to the rocket?

**S:** We believe it fell to Earth in the Arctic ocean north of Canada. There are no reports of any damage or injury.

**R2:** What were you trying to do with the sails? What was the mission?

**S:** As you know, our main goal is to send a space-sailing vehicle to the edge of our solar system—and maybe even farther than that. But really this vehicle wasn't supposed to do that. It was like a small-scale test. We wanted to get the rocket, or rather the capsule on top of the rocket, into orbit. Then it would release the sailing vehicle, and put that into orbit too. Then while it was going around the Earth, we would practice controlling the sails— turning them, folding them in and out, and so on. All by electronic signals of course. There is no person on that vehicle.

**R1:** How do space sails work?

**S:** Well, I've got to say first that no one has ever really launched a space-sailing vehicle. We know how they should work, but we've never tested it in real life.

**R1:** OK. How are they supposed to work?

**S:** It's actually really simple. Believe it or not, light can push things. It contains little packets of energy called photons, and when photons hit the space sail they push it along. The idea is to stretch the space sail out, like a big kite, and let the light from the sun push it through space.

**R2:** Is this the "solar wind" we hear about?

**S:** No. I'm glad you brought that up. No, solar wind is totally different. Just think "light." The sails are light, and they are pushed by light.

**R2:** So, if the sails get really far from the sun and the light gets weak, do they just stop? No light, no push, right?

**S:** Another good question. First of all, when it's close to the sun a space sail will pick up a lot of speed. We guess that it will be going about 100,000 miles per hour by the time it reaches the neighborhood of the outer planet Neptune. And since there's very little matter in space to slow it down, it should go a long way without any new push. But you are right. We have to find ways to get light from non-Sun resources to keep those sails traveling. One idea is to put a laser on a moon of Saturn and then shoot laser light at the sail. But what about beyond that? I don't know. We probably have to develop a system that will detect other light sources far out in space and then turn the sails to catch those photons.

**R1:** Just wondering. You used a Russian rocket. And you launched from some place…well, I don't know where it is, but it's not in the U.S. Why? Aren't you an American company?

**S:** We are an American company. We have our headquarters in Alabama. But we also have offices in lots of other countries. About that rocket, it was the best we could buy for the money we had. There's nothing wrong with American rockets…or with French rockets or whatever…but we can't afford them. And getting permission in the United States to launch a private rocket is really tough. The island in the Barents Sea was our best, cheapest, and safest alternative.

# Unit 12

**M = Marta**          **P = Professor Gleason**

**M:** Excuse me, Professor Gleason. Do you have a minute?

**P:** Sure…uh…I'm sorry. I don't remember your name.

**M:** I'm Marta. That's all right. I know you have hundreds of students.

**P:** So, how can I help you?

**M:** I'm really enjoying our discussion of Winston Churchill, but I'm having trouble with information I'm getting from all sorts of sources. I know he was a great prime minister but the other things…I…I honestly can't tell the difference between true stories and…well…I don't know. Fiction, I guess.

**P:** Actually, you're very smart to ask about that. A lot of students just accept everything they hear and don't question it. There is a lot of popular nonsense about him. What have you heard?

**M:** Uh… OK. Like some people say he was a soldier all over the place—Cuba, India, South Africa. And I know nobody could be everywhere like that.

**P:** Hmm. I can see how that seems unlikely, but really all that's true. And more. You could have mentioned Sudan, too. You have to remember how upper-class British men lived in the late 19th century. Churchill went to a military academy, Sandhurst, and it was sort of expected that he would serve in at least some part of the British Empire. I'll admit he got around a lot more than usual, but…

**M:** And that he was a best-selling author, too?

**P:** He was. *History of the English-Speaking Peoples* is the big one. He won the 1953 Nobel Prize in Literature.

**M:** Oh, come on. Really? How could anybody…

**P:** He was really, really talented. I'm serious. Whether you like his politics or not, you have to admire his abilities. Also, we have to remember that he had loads of servants, so his life was not full of the little daily chores you and I have to attend to. But that's not to say he was afraid of work. You know, he did most of the brickwork on a little playhouse for his daughter Mary.

**M:** Wow. What about all these quotes we hear about? It seems like every clever saying comes from him or…

**P:** Or George Bernard Shaw, or Mark Twain.…I know. That gets a little ridiculous. He didn't say everything that people credit him with. But he was very clever, and some…

**M:** How about, "I have nothing to offer but blood, sweat, and tears?"

**P:** Yes, that one is his, from 1940, although it's really, "blood, toil, tears, and sweat." But I don't know about a lot of others.

**M:** Like where this party guest criticizes his drinking, says she'd fill his cup with poison if he were her husband…?

**P:** And he says, "Madam, if you were my wife, I'd drink it?" Honestly, Marta. I don't know. It sounds like him, but I can't really say.

**M:** Thanks, Professor. I guess maybe he was a lot more accomplished than I thought.

**P:** I know it's hard to believe. A real Renaissance man!

198 Madison Avenue
New York, NY 10016 USA

Great Clarendon Street, Oxford OX2 6DP UK

Oxford University Press is a department of the University of Oxford.
It furthers the University's objective of excellence in research, scholarship,
and education by publishing worldwide in

Oxford  New York

Auckland  Cape Town  Dar es Salaam  Hong Kong  Karachi  Kuala Lumpur
Madrid  Melbourne  Mexico City  Nairobi  New Delhi  Shanghai  Taipei
Toronto

With offices in

Argentina  Austria  Brazil  Chile  Czech Republic  France  Greece  Guatemala
Hungary  Italy  Japan  Poland  Portugal  Singapore  South Korea  Switzerland
Thailand  Turkey  Ukraine  Vietnam

OXFORD and OXFORD ENGLISH are registered trademarks of
Oxford University Press in certain countries.

© Oxford University Press 2010

Database right Oxford University Press (maker)

**No unauthorized photocopying**

Any websites referred to in this publication are in the public domain and
their addresses are provided by

Oxford University Press for information only. Oxford University Press
disclaims any responsibility for the content.

Editorial Director: Laura Pearson
Publishing Manager: Erik Gundersen
Managing Editor: Louisa van Houten
Development Editor: Tracey Gibbins
Design Director: Susan Sanguily
Design Manager: Maj-Britt Hagsted
Associate Design Manager: Michael Steinhofer
Image Editor: Trisha Masterson
Design Production Manager: Stephen White
Senior Manufacturing Coordinator: Eve Wong
Production Coordinator: Elizabeth Matsumoto

ISBN: 978 019 472787 7

Printed in China

This book is printed on paper from certified and well-managed sources.

10  9  8

ACKNOWLEDGMENTS
The authors and publisher are grateful to those who have given permission to
reproduce the following extracts and adaptations of copyright material:
p52 "The Thrill Seeker" reproduced from Radio Times Magazine, 2–9 July
2004; p70 Philippa Forrester's "My First Crash" as told to Mark Anstead,
published 4 July 2004 in The Sunday Times. Reproduced by kind permission.

Although every effort has been made to trace and contact copyright holders
before publication, this has not been possible in some cases. We apologize for any
apparent infringement of copyright and if notified, the publisher will be pleased
to rectify any errors or omissions at the earliest opportunity.

Illustrations by: p6 Richard Jolley/www.CartoonStock.com; p7 Gill Button;
p13 Patrick Hadin/www.CartoonStock.com (restaurant); p16 Marc Tyler
Nobleman/www.CartoonStock.com; p29 Exley Publications, Fiffy's Guide to
Husbands/Helen Exley/Exley Publications Ltd.; p34 Michael Maslin/
The Cartoon Bank; p36 Harry Venning; p37 www.CartoonStock.com;
p46 Paul Gilligan/Getty Images; p56 Roger Penwill; p67 Ned Joliffe; p69 Harry
Venning (cars); p69 Harry Venning (insomniac/cow/homeless/piano/hotel);
p72 Matt Percival/www.CartoonStock.com

The publishers would like to thank the following for permission to reproduce
photographs:
Commissioned Photography:
p32 Pierre d'Alancaisez
Cover Photography:
Pixtal/AGE Fotostock: (top left); Photo Alto/Jupiter Images: James Hardy
(top center); dbimages/Alamy: Roy Johnson (top right); PhotoAlto/AGE
Fotostock/: Vincent Hazat (left center); Masterfile: (right center); Masterfile:
(bottom right); ASP/Getty Images: Kirstin Scholtz (bottom left)
Stock Photography:
p3 WestEnd61/Rex Features (woman); p3 Peter Adams Photography Ltd/
Alamy (pier ); p4/5 JoongAng Ilbo; p5 JoongAng Ilbo (Thomas/classmates);
p8 Image Source/Alamy; p9 Thinkstock Images/Comstock Images/Getty
Images; p10 John van Hasselt/Corbis UK Ltd.; p10/11 Goodshot/Punchstock;
p11 Corey Rich Photography; p13 imagesource/Punchstock (argument);
p14 WestEnd61/Rex Features; p15 Morgan David De Lossy/Corbis UK Ltd.;
p17 Photodisc/Punchstock; p19 Moviestore Collection Ltd.; p20 Image Source/
Punchstock; p21 PhotoSpin, Inc/Alamy; p22 Blend Images/Trevor Lush/
Getty Images; p23 Ian Hodgson/Corbis UK Ltd.; p24 Reuters/Corbis UK Ltd.
(Abagnale); p24 Dreamworks/Kobal Collection (crew); p25 Dreamworks/
Kobal Collection; p26 Jean Louis Batt/Taxi/Getty Images; p27 Charles Sykes/
Rex Features; p28 SNAP/Rex Features; p30 TMI/Alamy (woman); p30 Terry
Harris Just Greece Photo Library/Alamy (Hollywood); p30 Digital Vision/
Punchstock (daydreaming); p31 Image Source/Alamy; p33 S. Prezant/Corbis
UK Ltd. (beard); p33 T. McGuire/Corbis UK Ltd. (pencil); p33 MJ Cardenas
Photography/Getty Images (cooking); p35 imageshop/Punchstock;
p38 Photodisc/Oxford University Press; p38/39 Viesti Associates; p40 Jessica
Rinaldi/Reuters/Corbis UK Ltd.; p41 Medioimages/Punchstock;
p43 Blend Images/Alamy; p44 Capital Pictures; p45 Rhoda Peacher (coins);
p45 Image Bank/Getty Images (office); p47 Ghislain & Marie David De Lossy/
The Image Bank/Getty Images; p48 Richard Cooke/Alamy (Concorde);
p48 Jacques Jangoux/Alamy (falls); p48 Mary Winch/Axiom (towers);
p49 Travel-Shots/Alamy; p51 Gerrit Buntrock/Anthony Blake/Photolibrary
Group (cake); p51 Steve Meddle/Rex Features (Glastonbury); p52 Geoff
Mackley (crater/storm); p53 Photodisc/Oxford University Press (sheep); p53
Corbis/Punchstock (camping); p54 Rainer Jensen/Dpa/Corbis UK Ltd.; p55
Horizon International Images Limited/Alamy; p58 Oxford University Press
(friends); p58 Radius Images/Alamy (woman); p60 Tetra Images/Alamy
(newspaper); p60 RNZAF/Getty Images (iceberg); p61 Fogstock/Alamy;
p62 Photodisc/Oxford University Press; p63 Andrey Semenov/Alamy;
p65 NASA (mars); p65 Northrup Grumman/Ames Research Center/NASA
(probe); p66 Brand X/Punchstock; p69 Radius Images/Alamy (Stephanie);
p69 Charles Gullung/Corbis UK Ltd. (Don); p69 Image Source/Corbis UK
Ltd. (April); p70 Nils Jorgensen/Rex Features (Philippa); p70 image100/
Punchstock (screaming); p74 IT Stock/Punchstock; p75 LWA-JDC/Corbis
UK Ltd.; p76 Corbis UK Ltd.; p77 Steve Austin/Alamy; p78 Sipa Press/Rex
Features; p80 IT Stock/Punchstock

Spotlight on Testing:
pp3, 11, 19 (Hispanic female/Fancy/Veer AGE Fotostock);
pp5, 13, 21 (Hispanic male/ StockByte/AGE Fotostock/George Doyle);
pp7, 15, 23 (Asian female/ Tetra Images/ArtLifeImages/Superstock);
pp9, 17, 25 (Caucasian male/ Westend61/ArtLifeImages/Superstock/
HannoKeppel)